Using Focus Groups in Research

Lia Litosseliti

LONDON • NEW YORK

Continuum

The Tower Building   15 East 26th Street
11 York Road   New York
London SE1 7NX   NY 10010

British Library Cataloguing-in-Publication Data
A catalogue record for this book is available from the British Library.

ISBN: 0-8264-6472-6 (paperback)

Typeset by YHT Ltd, London
Printed and bound in Great Britain by MPG Books Ltd, Bodmin, Cornwall

Contents

Contents

Series Editor's Introduction

The Continuum Research Methods series aims to provide undergraduate, Masters and research students with accessible and authoritative guides to particular aspects of research methodology. Each title looks specifically at one topic and gives it in-depth treatment, very much in the tradition of the Rediguide series of the 1960s and 1970s.

Such an approach allows students to choose the books that are most appropriate to their own projects, whether they are working on a short dissertation, a medium-length work (15–40,000 words) or a fully-fledged thesis at MPhil or PhD level. Each title includes examples of students' work, clear explication of the principles and practices involved, and summaries of how best to check that your research is on course.

In due course, individual titles will be combined into larger books and, subsequently, into encyclopaedic works for reference.

The series will also be of use to researchers designing funded projects, and to supervisors who wish to recommend in-depth help to their research students.

Richard Andrews

Acknowledgements

Above all, I am indebted to those who have participated in and contributed to my focus groups, for being willing to share their experiences and for teaching me a lot about research.

I am grateful to my students, colleagues and friends for their insight and advice. I would particularly like to thank those researchers who responded to a questionnaire aimed at exploring the common views and hands-on experiences of focus group research, and Markus Perkmann for commenting on drafts of this book.

Special thanks to Shields Russell and Pepi Aggelopoulou for their unfailing encouragement, love and support over the years.

1

Introducing Focus Groups

In this first section, I offer a broad introduction to focus groups by looking briefly at definitions and mentioning some of the key aspects of the methodology, such as the different kinds of groups, composition and moderation. The section also places focus groups as a valuable qualitative research method in the social sciences, and raises some of the issues involved in using them within and outside the social sciences. Finally, examples of research using focus groups are given.

Preliminaries and definitions

Focus groups are small structured groups with selected participants, normally led by a moderator. They are set up in order to explore specific topics, and individuals' views and experiences, through group interaction. Focus groups are special groups in terms of purpose, size, composition and procedures. We can describe a focus group as 'a carefully planned discussion designed to obtain perceptions on a defined area of interest in a permissive, non-threatening environment' (Krueger 1994, p.6), where participants share and respond to comments, ideas and perceptions. It is important that those taking part find the discussion comfortable and enjoyable, do not feel pressurized to make decisions or reach consensus, and are encouraged to express different points of view. Groups are *focused* in the sense that they involve some kind of collective activity around a small number of issues (such as debating particular questions, reading a text, etc.), and are *interactive* in that the group forces and dynamics are of utmost importance. Participants respond to and build on the views expressed by others in the group – a synergistic approach that produces a range of opinions, ideas and experiences, and thus generates insightful information. It is these elements of a collective activity or socially-oriented event, together with the centrality of interaction, that make focus group methodology potentially invaluable for many social research projects (Gibbs 1997, Kitzinger 1994, Catterall and Maclaren 1997).

Focus groups offer some advantages compared to other methods of collecting data, such as interviews and participant observation. They present a more natural environment than an individual interview, as focus group participants 'are influencing and influenced by others – just as they are in real life' (Krueger 1994, p.19). Also, individual interviews focus on individual beliefs and attitudes, and can be more easily controlled by the interviewer than focus groups, which aim to obtain multiple views and attitudes, and often require complex negotiation of the on-going interaction processes among participants.

Further, focus groups may be seen to occupy a middle ground between participant observation and in-depth interviewing (Morgan 1997). Depending on the research goals and design, they can be used with an emphasis either on intervention or, as is most often the case in the social sciences, on observation. An emphasis on intervention may entail more formal and structured groups that can be seen as representative, while an emphasis on observation may result in exploratory, qualitative, naturalistic or interpretative groups. Focus group methodology is a form of group interviewing (indeed, this is the term used by social scientists before the 1980s), with a semi-structured questioning approach which relies on participants' responses. What distinguishes focus groups, however, from the broader category of group interviews is an emphasis on the interaction and the explicit use of such interaction as research data (Kitzinger 1994). Contrary to group interviewing, where a number of people are being interviewed at the same time and the emphasis is on the exchanges between the researcher and the participants, focus groups rely primarily on interaction and stimulation among the group participants themselves (Morgan 1997, Gibbs 1997). This stimulation is initially based on topics supplied by the researcher, but soon uncovers new, open-ended pathways for discussion.

Focus groups typically consist of between six and ten participants, but the size can range from as few as four (mini focus groups; see Kitzinger 1995 for an example) to as many as twelve (see Goss and Leinbach 1996), depending on the research purposes. Larger groups are difficult to manage, moderate and analyse successfully, but occasionally groups with more than ten participants can be useful for brainstorming. Smaller groups are more appropriate if the aim is to explore complex, controversial, emotional topics, or to encourage detailed accounts. Small groups offer more opportunity for people to talk and are more practical to set up and manage, as they can easily take place in less formal settings, such as homes and restaurants. The selection of participants is discussed in Section 3 but, generally speaking, to ensure a flowing discussion and a diversity of perspectives, it is useful to have at least six participants for the initial focus group.

I refer to the 'initial' group because, in most cases of focus group research, there will be more than one focus group, with different groups of people working on the same topic. This is because the outcome of any single session may not be telling enough, and also because focus groups require several representative users. In the past, researchers have organized one meeting with each of several focus groups, or a number of meetings with the same group. The number of groups used will depend on a variety of factors – primarily on the topic and the range of responses to the topic required, but also on the breadth of the target population and on the location of the groups. A typical number is between four and six groups. Many projects use a larger number, while the minimum of groups set up is usually three. It is too risky to build a research project around a single focus group, as this would make only limited claims about that particular group of people, and could hinder both comparative and in-depth exploration of the topic. It is also worth pointing out that each group in a series of focus groups will vary from the next. One group may be exciting and energetic, another may be low-key with reluctant participants, while another may be affected in unexpected ways by a dominant group participant attempting to take over the discussion. Sections 4 and 5 consider such factors and propose relevant useful strategies for developing questions and running groups effectively.

Each group would normally be composed of 'homogeneous, like-minded individuals from the same gendered, ethnic, sexual, economic or cultural background', though it is often beneficial to have 'participants from diverse backgrounds, as it maximises the possibility of exploring subjects from different perspectives' (Kitzinger 1995, 300). Although homogeneous groups, with similar needs and interests, work best for most focus group projects, this is not necessarily the case for all social science projects. Section 3 offers a detailed discussion of focus group composition, selecting participants and a moderator, and other practical aspects of focus group research. Generally speaking, a focus group may typically last between one and a half to two hours, and sessions are tape recorded (audio/video) to facilitate analysis.

Focus groups are facilitated by a moderator, who guides the discussion using a number of predetermined and carefully developed open-ended questions, with minimal intervention. The moderator maintains the group's focus, and ensures that the key questions are discussed, the discussion develops and the participants do not shift away from the topic of discussion or dominate it. To moderate a group successfully requires considerable planning and a moderator with good communication, managing and interpersonal skills. For example, a good moderator will keep the discussion on track without inhibiting the flow of ideas, will ensure that all group participants contribute, and will be able to probe participants while avoiding leading or 'closed' questions. It should be acknowledged that, as with any method where there is communication between the researcher and the participants, the data produced will be influenced by the presence, role, and perceived background of the moderator, and the actual interaction between the moderator and the participants. In order to minimize bias and the risk of manipulation from both the moderator and the participants, careful consideration needs to be given to how much the participants are told about the nature of the research, how leading is the moderator's input, and on how openly participants relate to one another and to the moderator (see Sections 3–5).

What kind of focus group?

As with other methods, the research questions and objectives of a study will determine what kind of focus group(s) will be appropriate. Projects in the social sciences typically involve full focus groups comprising between six and ten people, or mini focus groups with four to six participants. In marketing research, where focus groups have been and remain a prominent methodology, it is not uncommon to use telephone focus groups (involving four to six people), video-conference focus groups, and online focus groups (with 15–20 participants).

Focus groups that are not conducted in person may be less appropriate for social science research, and I would suggest that in most cases it will be necessary to complement virtual groups with live ones. Telephone, video and online focus groups can lack the richness, spontaneity and creativity of in-person focus groups. The advantages of virtual groups, such as participation over distances, savings on time and cost, and a speedier turnaround (for example, there is no need for transcription with online groups) are likely to be greater for market researchers and industry researchers focusing on products and services, than for social scientists involved in academic research. For the majority of social research projects, these advantages are offset by disadvantages, such as the lack of spontaneity, the loss of body language and the limited depth of response. The non-verbal communication among participants signals people's responses, opinions, alertness, interest in the topic and so on, and is therefore crucial. Equally important is the depth of response, as research results are not based on isolated responses, but rather on a web of responses and how these are pursued, grounded and clarified through group interaction. Non-verbal communication, depth and manner of response are complex elements of interaction, and this becomes especially evident at the stage of interpreting the results of focus group data, at which point the researcher is often overwhelmed by the difficulty of adequately capturing such complexity.

Online focus groups, in particular, can have additional disadvantages. They are not appropriate for exploring very complex concepts or for projects which require a high degree of confidentiality. These groups also rely on participants having access to the Internet, and – contrary to common perceptions – that still remains a specific and limited group of people. On the positive side, however, online focus groups can be seen as giving quiet or less confident participants opportunities to contribute more to the discussion than they would in person, and particularly in relation to sensitive or controversial topics (for example, drug abuse). In addition, online focus group interviewing may be the only option for some research projects with hard-to-reach individuals, such as busy professionals and executives, physicians, or government officials (Stewart and Shamdasani 1990).

In one example, online focus groups were used as a supplementary methodology at an early phase of a research project, prior to using additional questionnaire and in-depth interview methods (Rezabek 2000). The role of this particular focus group research was to formulate, through discussion with a number of 'experts' in distance and adult education who lived in different parts of the USA, key issues and questions that would then be explored through a questionnaire and indepth interviews with distance education students. These key issues were raised with the college learners in order to probe the motives, barriers and enablers in their decision to enrol on adult distance learning courses.

In this book, I am concentrating on in-person focus groups, although a lot of the basic elements will be useful – at least for the planning stage – for other kinds of groups. There are other appropriate sources of information for researchers working on projects for which telephone, video-conference, or online focus groups may be suitable (see Recommended Further Reading).

Focus groups as a qualitative research method in the social sciences

Focus groups have been extensively used in advertizing and market research, in political campaigning (for example, to explore people's reactions to wartime propaganda in the 1920s and 1930s) and as part of public policy and communications research (Krueger 1994, Morgan 1988, Merton 1987). More recently, focus groups have been used in education (e.g. Lederman 1990), linguistics (e.g. Myers 1998), health research (e.g. Kitzinger 1995; Powell and Single 1996), feminist research (e.g. Wilkinson 1998) and research on social movements and phenomena, such as racism and the environment.

The broader shift, since the 1980s, from quantitative to qualitative research methods has contributed to the increased use of focus groups by market researchers, mainly for the purposes of brand development and product evaluation. Academics use focus groups for a variety of different purposes (see Section 2 for a detailed discussion), and generally tend to rely on them to generate hypotheses and gain insight into participants' views, perceptions and attitudes on a given topic. Finally, political parties and policy makers in public, private and voluntary organizations use them to evaluate policy choices and alternatives and to explore public perceptions of policy matters. Other terms used to loosely describe focus group methodology are group discussions, focused interviews, citizen panels and sensitivity panels (Catterall and Maclaren 1997).

Despite being a socially-oriented research methodology with a central interest in interaction, focus groups are often underused or misused in the social sciences (Barbour and Kitzinger 1999; Gibbs 1997; Goss and Leinbach 1996; Lamnek 1995; Mayring 1993). One reason is that they are quite demanding to organize, conduct, moderate and analyse successfully – although they may often *appear* easier to use or less structured than other research methods. Another reason is the common perception that focus groups should not be used as the only source of data. While this may be an appropriate assumption in some cases, it certainly does not apply to all projects. Very often, however, this perception underlies more complex research designs, which rely on additional quantitative and qualitative methods in order to supplement focus group data. Typical examples are of focus groups preceding (as in the distance education example), following or being used at the same time as quantitative methods (for example, for triangulation and to clarify quantitative methods). At the same time, the more recent euphoria and increased interest in focus groups has meant that they are sometimes used in inappropriate situations (Morgan 1993) or in ad hoc ways. An example of this is organizations using what they call 'focus groups' in order to build consensus or resolve conflict; but these are not in any real sense focus groups if their purpose is other than collecting data (Morgan 1993). While focus groups may need to be adapted to special situations – such as by repeating periodic focus groups with the same participants, or conducting media focus groups – such changes must be clear and taken into consideration in the analysis of results (Krueger 1994). Focus groups are intended for gaining information and listening to people's views in a non-threatening environment – not to teach, inform, make decisions or resolve conflict (Krueger 1994).

A far more significant reason for not using rigorous focus group methodology in the social sciences is that the procedures, decisions, benefits and potential of this methodology have been inadequately discussed outside the context of advertizing or marketing research. While it may be appropriate in some marketing research to rely on focus groups in order to answer the question of 'what' kind of product would be successful, social scientists will typically put emphasis on exploring other complex questions about 'why' and 'how'. In turn, these questions make different assumptions about the research process and the research outcomes, and therefore require different methodological approaches, compared to questions about what kind of food will be bought by a consumer group or what proposals should be supported by a political party. Morgan describes the differences succinctly:

> For marketing research, the research environment outside of focus groups consists almost entirely of quantitative methods, while social scientists can rely on an active tradition of qualitative methods. The audience for marketing research is a bill-paying client, while social scientists address their colleagues in the form of a field of studies or a discipline. And, in marketing, the pragmatic pursuit of increased sales is the overwhelming goal, while social scientists pursue such nebulous goals as 'increased understanding'.   (Morgan 1988, p.77)

Moreover, market researchers in the past have tended to take group discussions at face value and to ignore the processes and dynamics of the interaction – and until recently, social scientists have been equally ignorant about paying necessary attention to these dynamics (Kitzinger 1994; Litosseliti and Sunderland 2002).

In addition to associating focus groups with questions in marketing and advertizing, then, the development of this methodology must be seen within the broader context of qualitative research, and the assumptions, aims and outcomes of qualitative methods. Simply put, qualitative methods are often applied to complex, rich-in-interpretation questions, and generally put emphasis on aspects of meaning, process, context: the 'why' and the 'how', rather than the 'how many' (Cohen and Manion 1994; Silverman 1993). Such methods are interested in language used in context, in meaning as it emerges from the participants themselves, rather than being predetermined by the researcher or measured by variables. These are all elements that are important in focus groups. Focus groups are a contextual and relatively non-hierarchical method, two features that are especially useful, for example, for feminist research (Wilkinson 1999). Further, in aiming to get to a deep and detailed understanding of broad patterns found among a group of participants within a social setting or social event, focus groups produce qualitative data. And importantly, focus groups elicit information in a way which allows researchers to find out *why* an issue is salient, as well as what is salient about it (Morgan 1988).

Krueger (1994) points out that the evolution of focus groups, and qualitative research methods in general, has been delayed as a result of a long-established preoccupation with quantitative procedures and assumptions about people, things and the nature of reality. The shift towards qualitative approaches can be viewed in the context of developments in post-structuralist and post-modernist theories, the importance of language or 'discursive turn' across the social sciences, and an understanding of our sense of self as multiple, fragmented and changing. These developments and themes can be traced across the social sciences: in anthropology, ethnology, education, economics, finance, commerce, social geography, law, philosophy, politics, linguistics, psychology, sociology, social policy, business, management, environmental sciences, government, media and cultural studies and gender studies. Within these, the shift towards qualitative procedures is part of an ongoing debate about moving away from *positivistic* paradigms of research (for example, positivism) towards more *interpretative* (for example, phenomenology, ethnomethodology, sociolinguistics and ethnography) and *critical* paradigms (for example, Marxism and feminism). Sarantakos (1998) provides a comprehensive discussion of these paradigms, and their similarities and differences. I would like to emphasize here that the 'discursive turn', with its emphasis on language use in context and on the dynamics and politics of interaction (see, among others, Litosseliti and Sunderland 2002), has contributed to the increasing importance of socially-oriented and interaction-oriented research methods, such as focus groups.

As with other qualitative methods where meaning emerges from the participants, focus groups have an element of flexibility and adaptability (in terms of the setting and the participants) which should not be mistaken for looseness. Their open-ended nature offers the benefit of allowing insight into the world of the participant in the participant's own language, but it takes a skilled and experienced researcher/moderator to successfully bring out and build on such insight (see Section 3 for a discussion of the role of the moderator). As mentioned above, focus groups present a challenge for the researcher and require a high level of knowledge and skill to be effective. This is in contradiction to some researchers' perception of focus groups as a quick and easy method for testing hypotheses (as discussed by Merton 1987) – a perception that may be based on misused or less rigorous applications of this method in time-intensive marketing or advertizing projects. But, as Steward and Shamdasani argue (1990), instead of ad hoc or atheoretical exercises, focus groups can be rigorous and useful social science research tools that are well grounded in theory. The following sections aim to support this view.

Before we look at some of the benefits and limitations of focus group methodology, let us consider some examples of research projects in the social sciences where focus groups have been used. There are numerous examples on a variety of topics and within areas such as linguistics, sociology, education, media and cultural studies, psychology and health, among others. The idea behind the following random list is simply to give some indication of the range of focus group use. Consider the following studies where focus groups have been used:

- Assessing the impact of advertisements before going public
- Exploring people's attitudes to issues such as consumerism, shoplifting and impulse buying
- Developing community education to prevent HIV/ AIDS (Munodawafa *et al.* 1995, for an example in Zimbabwe)
- Understanding the gap between education messages about teenage pregnancy and a community's beliefs about its causes, effects, and prevention
- Understanding the perceptual gap between the American public and government officials regarding US-Soviet relations
- Identifying the discursive construction of national identity in Europe, with particular attention to Austria (Wodak *et al.* 1999)
- Exploring how media messages are processed/how the media affect audience perceptions of HIV/AIDS (Kitzinger 1994, 1995)
- Investigating public perceptions of the environment and public responses to environmental communications

- Analysing rhetorics of environmental sustainability: how people talk about the environment in pubs, markets and on buses (Myers and Macnaghten 1998)
- Understanding people's construction of moral and gendered arguments on the topic of marriage (Litosseliti 1999, 2001)
- Exploring sustainable safe public spaces: understanding how heterosexuals and homosexuals use (safe) space according to their experience and perceptions of violence
- Studying the audiences of popular action films, people's ways of talking about going to the cinema, and how they are affected by public discourses of action films (Barker and Brooks 1998)
- Investigating public attitudes and sensibilities towards animals and biotechnology in contemporary Britain
- Looking at the construction of gender through conversation about violence, and the social reconstruction of gender in self-defence classes

These examples of studies can be better understood in the context of the kind of questions that can be succesfully addressed through focus groups (discussed in Section 2).

Summary

This section has introduced focus group methodology and some of its key elements, particularly within the context of the social sciences. It has shown that:

- Focus groups are special groups in terms of purpose, size, composition and procedures.
- Interaction in focus groups is of utmost importance.
- Different kinds of research require different kinds of focus groups.

- Focus group methodology has developed as a result of the broader shift from quantitative to qualitative research methods.
- Focus group methodology is important for qualitative research and can combine flexibility and adaptability with rigour and theoretical grounding.
- Focus groups are often underused or misused within the social sciences.

2

Benefits and Limitations of Focus Group Methodology

This section reviews some of the benefits and some of the limitations of focus groups, and looks at common pitfalls. The discussion that follows aims to provide insight into the kinds of questions or problems that this methodology can appropriately address.

When to use focus groups and for what kinds of questions

Focus group research is useful for revealing through interaction the beliefs, attitudes, experiences and feelings of participants, in ways which would not be feasible using other methods such as individual interviews, observation or questionnaires (Gibbs 1997). In contrast to such methods, focus groups can provide insight on multiple and different views and on the dynamics of interaction within a group context, such as consensus, disagreement and power differences among participants; in fact, it is common to obtain information on the power differences between the participants on the one hand and decision-makers or professionals on the other (for example patients and doctors, members of the public and government officials). In contrast to many other methods, focus groups are an appropriate method for obtaining information from illiterate communities. They also provide the opportunity to ask people to discuss their views about or approaches to activities that span many days or weeks, something that would take considerable amounts of time and resources to observe directly. Focus group methodology allows for flexibility in examining a range of topics with a variety of individuals, sometimes more directly and less expensively than, say, individual interviews.

Focus groups can be used as the primary source of data (a *self-contained* method), as a *supplementary* source of data, and in *multimethod* studies which combine data-gathering methods (Morgan 1997). A typical example of using focus groups as the primary source of data would be exploring people's attitudes to, say, consumerism, by running groups differentiated by gender, age, profession, etc. In conjunction with other methods, they can be used for validity checking of findings and triangulation between methods. Triangulation can be particularly useful when the topic of investigation is very complex or controversial, or requires a holistic view. For example, on the subject of teenage pregnancy, focus groups with women may be used in conjunction with analyses of media texts on the topic and interviews with those promoting sex education. Similarly, focus groups on the topic of marriage can be compared to controversial media arguments on the topic (Litosseliti 2001, 2002).

Focus groups can be used both during the preliminary or exploratory stages of a research project, where questions are explored and hypotheses generated, and at later stages for assessing the development, effectiveness or impact of a programme of activities. An example of the former is a project on 'Violence, Security and Space' (Skeggs, Moran and Truman, 1998–2000), where focus groups with gay men, lesbians and single women in a city and a rural area were used early in the project to explore these groups' perceptions of violence and space and thus determine the subsequent focus on one or more of these groups. An example of the latter use would be conducting focus groups with teachers, students and education officials to assess the effectiveness of an existing distance education programme. Finally, focus groups are appropriate for grounded theory development, where the aim is on the generation of – rather than the testing of – predetermined hypotheses and concepts (Kitzinger 1994).

The following list summarizes the main appropriate uses of focus group methodology, based on various academic discussions on the topic (Morgan 1988; Morgan and Krueger 1993; Krueger 1994; Race *et al.* 1994; Powell and Single 1996; Gibbs 1997).

Focus groups are useful for:

- *Discovering new information* (for example, about a new product) and *consolidating old knowledge* (for example, examining people's habits)
- Obtaining a number of *different perspectives* on the same topic, in participants' own words
- Gaining information on participants' *views, attitudes, beliefs, responses, motivations and perceptions* on a topic; *'why'* people think or feel the way they do
- Examining participants' *shared understandings* of everyday life, and the *everyday use of language and culture of particular groups*
- *Brainstorming and generating ideas,* with participants discussing different angles of a problem, and possibly helping to identify solutions
- Gaining insights into the ways in which individuals are influenced by others in a group situation (*group dynamics*)
- *Exploring controversial issues and complex or sensitive topics*

The importance of interaction in focus groups is evident from this list. Despite some artificiality, focus groups are unique in obtaining rich amounts of data and different perspectives on a topic through interaction. The direct, open-response interaction among participants and between the moderator and the participants allows for a variety of responses, clarification, probing, connections among points made, nuances and deeper levels of meaning (Stewart and Shamdasani 1990). Interaction is important not simply because it tells us things about people's views, values, language and so on, but also because it involves participants learning from each other and reconsidering or re-evaluating their own understandings and experiences (Kitzinger 1994, 1995). Participants will come to the focus group with both set and malleable opinions, and often their opinions will develop and shift as a result of the discussion.

Because of this process of sharing, asking, doubting and reconsidering, the researcher/moderator may have less control over the interaction and the data produced, compared to interviewing or quantitative studies (Morgan 1988). This can be a problem for less experienced researchers. However, with focus groups that are carefully planned and skilfully moderated, this lack of predetermination can be a strength rather than a limitation. As emphasized earlier, the benefits of allowing insight into the world of the participant in the participant's own language can outweigh the limitations, and is a priority for social research projects, many of which rely on a collaborative research process.

In addition, this emphasis on participants' own language and the process of developing and re-framing their views as a result of collaboration can be important for the participants themselves, who often find the focus group experience empowering. Gibbs (1997) points out that, although focus groups are not empowering for everybody (for instance, shy persons), many participants enjoy being actively involved in decision-making and what they

19

perceive as activities that can make a difference. It is also my experience that people often appreciate the opportunity to work collaboratively with researchers, and to have their opinions, knowledge and experiences valued. When conducting focus groups with people from a local small community, I found that participants were willing to volunteer to participate in a group, without immediate rewards, as long as they felt that the project was depending on our collaboration. Goss and Leinbach (1996) also found in their research that participants experienced a sense of emancipation through speaking in public and developing reciprocal relationships with the researchers.

Limitations of focus groups

Now that you have some ideas about the usefulness or suitability of focus group methodology, you can perhaps infer when focus groups should not be used in a study. As a general rule, focus groups should not be used on topics which are unfamiliar to the participants, which do not encourage different perspectives, and which may hinder free-flowing talk and interaction. Focus groups will not be appropriate if there is a mismatch between the researcher's topics of interest and the participants' ability to discuss these topics, and if group participants do not share at least some common characteristics in relation to the research topic (this is discussed in Section 3). They should also be avoided if there is not adequate time and resources for organizing and conducting the groups properly. Focus groups can be time-consuming and expensive, and a capable, experienced moderator is essential (see Section 3).

More importantly, however, you should not use focus groups unless you are aware of their important methodological limitations. The main limitations are summarized below, based on discussions by Krueger (1994), Morgan (1988, 1993) and Gibbs (1997).

Potential limitations of focus groups:

- *Bias and manipulation*: danger of leading participants and encouraging them to respond to your own prejudices; participants saying what they think you want to hear
- *'False' consensus*: some participants with strong personalities and/or similar views may dominate the discussion, while others may remain silent
- *Difficulty in distinguishing between an individual view and a group view*: groups sometimes appear more consistent than they are because individuals who disagree may not say so; groups often generate more emotion than any of the individual participants may feel about the issue; individual behaviour is subject to group influence
- *Difficulty in making generalizations* based on the focus group information (not only because of the limited number of participants, but also due to the difficulty of having a really representative sample)
- *Difficulty of analysis and interpretation of results* (due to the open-ended nature of focus groups, and the influence of many immediate situational factors)

Some of these limitations can be addressed through careful planning and skilful moderating of the groups (as discussed later in this book). Dominating participants can be dealt with through firm, yet non-intrusive, moderating, and with the help of a topic guide, in order to keep the discussion on track. The moderator will also set some rules of behaviour to be observed during the discussions: for example, asking people not to talk at the same time. Very careful selection of participants, in accordance with the research questions being explored, should help to avoid a disruptive mismatch among participants and between the topics set by the researcher and the participants' ability to discuss them. It is also essential to have a discussion with the participants beforehand about what is expected of them: for example, explaining that there are no right and wrong answers, and that they are not expected to reach consensus. Careful design of the questions and topics to be developed during the discussion, together with experience, will help the moderator to minimize bias, by avoiding the use of leading and yes/no questions, and by encouraging a balance of contributions among participants. To facilitate both with practical aspects and with the interpretation of results, it is also useful to have an additional person (an observer or assistant) present when conducting the focus group discussions (all these issues are explored in detail in Sections 3, 4 and 5).

As regards the issue of generalizability, while it is sometimes useful to use focus groups in conjunction with other research methods (for example, observation), it is crucial to acknowledge that results may not be generalizable or representative, but indicative: that is, illustrating particular social phenomena. This also applies to methods other than focus groups, including quantitative methods. Illustrating and exploring particular social phenomena in depth is precisely the aim and scope of many social projects, although it should be said that debates about validity in the social sciences are highly contested. Getting a representative sample of participants for a focus group presents an additional difficulty. It is true that certain types of participants, mainly extroverts, are more likely to take part in a focus group than people who are not very articulate or confident, or have communication problems or special needs (Gibbs 1997). But representativeness is difficult to achieve with many qualitative methods, and is immediately dependent on the aims and assumptions of the research undertaken. What is more important to emphasize is that caution must be taken in suggesting that focus groups can replicate how people communicate within other group settings. Krueger makes a good point on the question of validity of focus group results in concluding that 'focus groups are valid if they are used carefully for a problem that is suitable for focus group inquiry' (1994, p.31).

The potential bias and manipulation risk is related to the fact that focus groups can assess what participants *say* they do or believe, but not necessarily what they *actually* do or believe. A researcher involved in planning, conducting and analysing focus groups needs to be aware of entering the vague and difficult terrain of people's motivations. Participants may tell you what they think you want to hear, on the basis of their perception of your background and depending on what and how much they know beforehand about the research. They often do not want to tell certain things to a group of people, particularly if they perceive these things to be too personal or embarrassing, or they may think the language they want to use is inappropriate for that group setting. They may not be truthful or tell you half-truths, and the motives for this are likely to be both multiple and elusive, sometimes even for the participants themselves. You should anticipate that group members will often try to rationalize their behaviour and obscure sensitive issues: for example, they may not admit to lack of knowledge or they may hold back information that could cause them to lose face (for example, about status, money or certain values). Most people will also try to maintain a consistent version of what they are like – the moderator is not immune to this either! – which can be misleading, given that the same person typically does different things at different times and for different purposes.

The complexity of people's motivations is further

accentuated within groups, where participants act both as individuals and as members of the group. It is predictable that individual behaviour is influenced by group behaviour, and vice versa, although how exactly this happens is far from predictable for the interviewer. Some participants will be selective in what they say or will take specific positions because of others in the group, in the same way that people in general do not form opinions in isolation. Individual focus group participants speak in a specific context within a specific culture (Gibbs 1997), and it takes a good moderator to grasp the various contextual parameters and delve below what is said. A skilful moderator may achieve this by being alert to people's language, feelings, body language and visual cues; by creating an open, friendly, non-threatening environment for the discussion; by encouraging people to be forthcoming, particularly if some participants tend to be shy or avoid disagreement; and by gauging individual views, perceptions and emotions during one-to-one chats or interviews with each of the participants. I find post-discussion one-to-one interviews extremely useful, as it is often during these that people disclose personal or sensitive information.

There are other ways of achieving deeper understanding and going below the surface of what is said in focus groups, such as by holding a pilot focus group, so that you develop better knowledge of expected comments and attitudes, and by including group and individual questions that check participants' truthfulness during or after the discussions. Especially because focus groups can be used to explore *why* an issue is salient, as a researcher you have the resources available for better understanding the gap between what people say and what they do. If participants discuss a range of multiple understandings and meanings, then multiple explanations of participants' attitudes can be articulated (Gibbs 1997; Lankshear 1993).

On a more practical level, you need to be prepared for the considerable logistic effort and planning required for using focus groups effectively. I have mentioned that focus groups can be time-consuming, difficult to set up, conduct, and analyse, and – depending on the number of groups and the type of participants – expensive. It may prove difficult to recruit participants, get an appropriate venue, or obtain good recording equipment, and so you need to allow considerable time for the planning of these aspects of the research (see Section 3). Consider also the importance of requiring (and possibly recruiting) a moderator with many different skills and experience in group interview techniques (see Sections 3 and 4). Moreover, transcription, a long and difficult process in general, can be especially so in the case of focus groups, where there are many different voices in the recordings, and a huge amount of data involved. As with many other methods, analysis can present difficulties, as focus groups are open-ended and unpredictable, participants often modify their positions during the discussion, and all comments must be interpreted within the particular context of the group interaction (see Section 6 for a discussion of transcription and analysis issues). In short, ask yourself the following questions before embarking on a focus group project: Will there be enough time and resources to develop and apply this methodology? Do you have the skills necessary to plan, moderate and analyse your focus groups or will you need to recruit and work with others?

The most common pitfalls when making choices about focus group research concern the size and number of groups organized, the coverage of issues during the discussion, and the degree of structure and flexibility in moderating the groups. For example, having groups which are too large (with more than eight participants) will not necessarily lead to a broader or more 'representative' discussion; rather, it is likely to create difficulties in managing the discussion and the group dynamics (particularly if the moderator is not experienced), and result in less detailed, in-depth, or diverse accounts. Similarly, having too many groups can lead to redundancy, repetition, and significant organizational work; having too few groups can be equally problematic. While the first in a series of focus groups is likely to cover a broader area of issues, the subsequent focus groups can offer a deeper and sometimes comparative exploration of what is brought up in the first group. Trying to do too much in one group meeting usually means sacrificing the deeper focus on the quality of the information shared. It may also limit the opportunities for experimentation, examination of alternatives, and getting to the underlying beliefs and practices.

As regards moderating the groups, it is crucial to consider that the degree of structure and flexibility in moderating focus groups is an important decision that will affect the results. While some research projects require a more structured approach, I find that the most productive groups move away from the sequential question and answer model. Flexibility during the group discussions means allowing for the list of topics to be revised, the sequence of questions to be altered and, crucially, deciding there and then whether to pursue a point in more depth and detail. This requires a confident, observant, knowledgeable and skilled moderator. It is a common mistake to assume that, as researchers, we are the most suitable persons to moderate our focus groups. First, we need to assess our understanding of group dynamics our ability to extract, verify and develop information, and generally our communication, managing and interpersonal skills (see Section 3). Focus group research can be an exciting challenge for social researchers wanting to gain a different perspective on their field of interest; but focus groups have to be used appropriately to be a rewarding experience for the researcher and the participants (Gibbs 1997).

Summary

This section has focused on the benefits, limitations and problems involved with using focus groups in research.

- Focus groups are appropriate for gaining insight on multiple and different perspectives, interaction and power dynamics within a group, 'what' happens and 'why' it happens, controversial, sensitive and complex topics.
- Focus groups can be used as the primary or a supplementary source of data, during the exploratory or the later stages of a research project.
- Focus groups are good for generating new ideas and consolidating old knowledge.
- Focus groups require careful planning and a skilful moderator, in order to reduce the risk of bias/manipulation and 'false' consensus, to deal with dominating participants, distinguish among views, and delve beneath what people say.
- Focus group results are unlikely to be generalizable or representative.
- Focus groups require considerable logistic effort and resources.
- Common pitfalls in focus group research concern the size and number of groups organized, the coverage of topics, and the degree of structure and flexibility in moderating.

3

Planning and Organizing Focus Groups

This section outlines the process of planning focus group research, and the main factors to consider when recruiting participants, deciding on the role and skills of the moderator, and thinking about the practical and ethical aspects of the research.

Let us assume that you have decided to use focus groups as an appropriate methodology for the purposes of your research. As part of the planning of any research that involves groups, you will have to think of the goals of a group, the various tasks, the group size and composition (in terms of age, sex, status, ability, culture, personalities and so on), as well as of organizational aspects, such as access and resources. In the case of focus groups, planning is of utmost importance, and additional time and effort should be allowed for recruiting suitable participants and making decisions about the skills and the role of the moderator.

First, you need to be clear about the *research aims and purposes*, the *topic* or *issue* to be discussed, and the *anticipated outcomes*. For your research plan, you will need to write down the answers to these questions (adapted from Krueger 1994, p.43):

- Why do this study?
- What is the key topic, issue or problem about which information is needed?

- What kind of information will be produced and what is important information for this project?
- What is the anticipated outcome of the study?
- Who will use this information, how, and for what purposes?

Once you address these questions, you can start thinking about the 'how'. Your decisions on what kind of focus group is appropriate, with how many people, where, when and how often, will be determined by the research goals, the issue investigated, the information required and the outcomes anticipated. You can then begin to recruit appropriate participants and a moderator, if you are not planning to moderate the groups yourself. You will also have to consider various practical issues, such as access to people, time available, resources required and some important ethical issues (discussed later in this section). The diagram below represents this progression in the planning of the focus group research.

Research purpose	Research questions/ issues/ outcomes	Participants (who, why, where)	Moderator (who, how)	Resources/ Practical & Ethical issues (how, why)

Figure 3.1   Steps/decisions in the planning of a focus group

I cannot emphasize enough the benefits of doing a *pilot focus group* prior to running the actual focus group sessions. I have learned some important lessons and improved my planning of the actual groups by taking the extra time and effort to do this. For my pilot focus group in a research project looking at moral arguments on the topic of marriage (Litosseliti 1999), I aimed to recruit participants similar to those who would take part in the actual groups. This particular pilot group consisted of only four participants, as I was not interested in the sample as such, but in the kind of interaction and dynamics among the participants in general, and among the male and female participants in particular. I was also interested in discussing the research project afterwards with the pilot participants, and taking on board their insights and suggestions about the planned focus groups. The pilot focus group discussions proved extremely useful for testing and learning about the following:

1 *The content/key themes of the discussion and people's responses*
   Themes and responses on the topic of marriage included talk about politics, morality, class, religion and the mass media. Gender was discussed at length, in relation to topic areas such as stereotyping, sexism, single mothers and the exploitation of women, and so were values, particularly 'individualistic' and 'collective' moral values. These themes and participants' responses to them helped me to plan the topic guide (see Section 4), not simply in terms of indicating what topics to cover, but also in throwing light on which topics were likely to be vague, complex or lead to conflict, and which could take longer for participants to tackle. This information led to some alteration of the sequencing of questions, the wording of questions and the planned timings.

2 *The dynamics of the interaction*
   Although focus groups are generally unpredictable, a pilot group can minimize this unpredictability by illustrating some of the dynamics of interaction that may also appear in the actual focus groups. For example, I was able to anticipate, to a certain extent, how the flow of the interaction changed depending on the questions asked and on their wording. I found out

whether the questions were understood easily and whether they encouraged discussion. I learned that some questions and some probes were more effective than others: for example, I discovered that asking 'why' questions put some participants in a defensive position, or led them to provide any answer, even an inaccurate one. In addition, I had the opportunity to practise techniques of dealing with dominating speakers, to listen to the discussion and my own moderating on tape, and to include in the research plan details I had missed or not thought about.

3 *The mechanics of the discussion*
The pilot focus group offered ample opportunity to test some practical aspects of the discussion, such as the room arrangement and seating positions; the quality of recorded sound; and participants' reactions to being recorded.

Finally, the pilot focus group allowed me to make more informed decisions about the research design, in particular highlighting how changing parts of the design can affect all the above aspects of the discussion: content, dynamics and mechanics. For example, it became evident that in this case asking participants to look at materials relating to the topic at the beginning of the discussion was not a good idea: asking the pilot participants to read an article from the *Guardian* newspaper on the topic of marriage resulted in them limiting their arguments to those used by the two writers in that particular text. This made it very difficult to explore the participants' own views and strategies around the topic, as the focus shifted from the participants' interaction to a critique and reflection on the newspaper debates. Consequently, for the planning of the actual focus groups, I decided to let participants talk about the topic, and not introduce the newspaper article until near the end of the discussion.

The article would then act as a tool for summarizing points in the debate, encouraging additional reactions, and allowing participants to reflect on what they had shared up to that point.

Selecting the participants

Focus groups are normally made up of people with certain common characteristics and similar levels of understanding of a topic, rather than aiming for diversity. This is because, in general, people tend to express personal views and disclose more to those whom they perceive as similar to them in certain ways, than to those who differ from them (Morgan 1988; O'Brien 1993; Krueger 1994). Krueger illustrates this with the example of long-distance travellers on a plane or bus, who are prepared to casually share personal information about themselves with the person seated next to them. He points out that such self-disclosure takes place because 'one or both of the travellers may have sensed that they are alike' (in terms of age, sex, occupation or attitudes on a topic), and because it is a non-threatening environment, given that the persons 'will likely never see each other again' (1994, p.13).

The common characteristics among focus group participants will depend on the focus and specific purpose of the research: who do you want to hear from? They usually consist of both *demographic characteristics*, such as age, sex, educational background, race, ethnicity, education level, income or professional status, and *knowledge or familiarity with the given topic*. For example, if the purpose of the research is to examine perceptions about a certain destination, it may be important to have one group that has visited it before, and another group who have not. Similarly, in a project on animals and biotechnology, groups targeted may include farmers, hunters, pet owners and animal rights activists. This is an example of homogeneity being broadly defined, not necessarily targeting a specific age group or a certain occupation. For my focus group research on moral arguments about marriage, groups needed to be defined more narrowly: it was important to have male and female participants who had never married and participants who had, as well as both 'lay' and academic perspectives, in order to achieve a diversity of experiences that relied on and gave rise to a variety of moral arguments (Litosseliti 2001, 2002). The homogeneity of a group, therefore, will be more important and more narrowly defined for some projects than others, particularly if the topic is sensitive. For example, in the 'Violence, Security, Space' project (Skeggs, Moran and Truman 1998–2000), it was important to have separate groups of gay men, lesbians and heterosexuals in order to ensure a supportive environment for discussion, and particularly for openly sharing sensitive information about sexuality, safety and violence.

Overall, as a researcher you will need to be constantly aware that differences in terms of gender, age, class, or professional and 'lay' perspectives can make a significant impact on people's contributions and on the degree of cohesiveness in the group. A substantial body of research in social psychology, which looks at people's behaviour in groups (see Stewart and Shamdasani 1990 for a detailed discussion), points to certain individual characteristics and, consequently, group dynamics that are important in the planning of research involving groups. These are typically physical, personality and demographic characteristics. For example, it is suggested that people's social contacts, ability to empathize, leadership behaviour and conformity increase with age, while a tendency to interrupt and take risks decreases (Stewart and Shamdasani 1990). There is also evidence that women interrupt less than men in mixed-sex groups, and are more concerned with creating rapport and coherence in the group. In addition, there are studies discussing the difference individuals' physical characteristics can make in a group situation: for instance, attractive people are often perceived as more knowledgeable (Stewart and Shamdasani 1990).

In practice, you will need to strike a balance between similarity and difference as regards potential participants, as often too homogeneous a group may result in fewer diverse opinions and experiences (Gibbs 1997). This may mean deciding on participants who are homogeneous in some respects while not compatible in others: for example, homogeneous in terms of socioeconomic status but incompatible in terms of gender. The research question(s) being investigated will determine these parameters; if the research question is related to the responses of certain types of individuals, for example, women, teachers, older and younger people, the focus group composition will reflect this type of individual. In one example of a three-year research project on 'Global Citizenship and the Environment' (Myers, Szerszynski and Urry 1996–99), part of which explored how global citizenship might enter into people's everyday lives, focus group participants were chosen from urban and rural areas on the basis of their more global experience (for example, corporate managers) and their more local experience (for example, women active in local organizations, and men who owned small shops).

During selection of focus group participants for a project, you also need to be alert to subtle, not always apparent, distinctions within each 'category' of participants, such as social and occupational status, income and educational level (Krueger 1994). It is obvious that groups of students, hospital workers, single mothers, farmers, etc., while having some things in common, will not be homogeneous. Among a group of, for example, randomly selected single mothers, there may be women with higher levels of prosperity or education than others. As a result, the group may be 'hesitant to share', and may 'defer their opinions' to those perceived to be more knowledgeable or influential (Krueger 1994). The issue here is not who actually has power, but who is *perceived* to have the social power and hence the ability to influence others in a group situation. To extend the above example, it is problematic to assume that any one individual can be representative of their gender, culture or race. As a researcher, you must think about such distinctions and assumptions carefully before and during the process of recruiting participants. During the actual sessions, you may want to signal the importance of commonality to the participants, by telling them that they have been selected because they share particular experiences related to the topic.

Special attention should be given to selecting participants for focus groups employed in studies seeking to understand a 'communication or understanding gap between groups or categories of people' (Krueger 1994, p.44), particularly between more and less powerful groups. Examples of such research include focus groups with policy-makers and the public, physicians and patients, employers and employees. Such studies can be extremely valuable in demystifying unequal relations of power, resolving related problems and making certain groups more visible. It is important, however, that those perceived to be more knowledgeable or influential (for example, senior professionals in the medical, education, business and scientific professions) are not recruited in the same group as those people employed, treated or taught by them. Depending on the research questions and aims of a project, separate groups will be needed for teachers and students, doctors and patients, employers and employees, and, broadly speaking, for 'experts' and the general public. To take a rather predictable example, during a series of focus groups in the USA, a gap was found between how economists and how the public perceived the economy and interpreted economic signs. While the experts wanted policies that increased productivity and growth, the public perceived a healthy economy as one where everyone has a job (*Business and Higher Education Report*, 1991, cited in Krueger 1994).

In addition, it is wise not to mix in the same group individuals with different lifestyles or who are at different stages in their life (for example, students and professionals, or women who work outside the home and those who do not), unless the topic necessitates such composition. Researchers sometimes also recommend against mixing gender in focus groups. There is some evidence that this can lead to greater conformity in the group (see Stewart and Shamdasani 1990); but the main problem seems to be the tendency for men to dominate the discussion, to 'speak more frequently and with more authority when in groups with women' – what is sometimes referred to as the 'peacock effect' (Krueger 1994, p.78). However, participants who tend to dominate the discussion cannot necessarily be avoided in single sex groups, and for many projects mixed-sex groups will be necessary. In my research, for example, where gender was salient and mixed-sex interaction/argumentation of essence, it was important to have both male and female participants in each focus group (Litosseliti 1999).

A fair amount has been written about recruiting complete strangers as focus group participants. The assumption has been that if there is no history and relationship between the participants before or after the session, they will be more likely to share information freely and openly. This has been particularly desirable for focus groups in market research, and is possible in cases where it is practical to recruit strangers, such as in big cities.

Different projects, however, require different approaches. In many community studies, it may not only be impractical to recruit complete strangers (because participants need to come from a small area), but also undesirable: for example, when the research seeks to explore the opinions of local residents (Krueger 1994). In other words, recruiting people acquainted with one another may be consistent with the objectives of the research, but caution is needed with groups of people who have significant contact with each other: friends, relatives and colleagues. Friends can affect group cohesion, engage in private conversations, inhibit other participants, and endorse each other's views (Templeton 1987). Spouses can end up assuming the roles of the talkative partner and the quiet or silent partner. Familiarity can limit self-disclosure and discourage disagreement, as interaction is likely to rely more on past experiences, shared or assumed knowledge, and particular events, rather than on diverse perspectives on the immediate topic (Myers 1998).

Recruiting participants for focus groups can be a difficult and time-consuming process, depending on the topic and the group targeted. While market researchers may rely on databases and telephone screening, researchers in the social sciences will usually look for participants where they are most likely to be found (for example, students can be recruited in classes, bars and halls of residence). They may also rely on advertizing, face-to-face contact, key informants, existing social networks and word of mouth. Specifying a target audience will depend, as discussed earlier, on the purposes of the research, and on the target group's identifiable and distinctive features, as dictated by those purposes. It will also depend on the research budget; if this allows for only a limited number of focus groups, these need to be targeted and planned even more carefully. Once those decisions are made, and there is a pool of potential participants, a good general rule is to select individuals who are likely to be participative as well as reflective.

It is common practice, particularly in the commercial world but also in academic research, to provide a monetary incentive for focus group participants. This serves as a stimulus for people to take part, acknowledges their time and effort, and indicates that the focus group is important. Depending on the length of the discussion and the type of social group from which participants are recruited, a monetary incentive can range from £20 to £60 (ideally in cash) per session for each participant. Alternative incentives may include refreshments and a free lunch, book vouchers and gifts. Travel expenses may have to be paid in addition to these, and for some groups it will be important to provide baby-sitting facilities on the day of the meeting. Krueger (1994) observes that in a number of situations it will be nearly impossible to conduct focus groups without incentives. However, in my experience particularly of academic small-scale research projects, people are often willing to participate in a focus group without a monetary incentive. This is especially the case when people are interested in the topic of discussion, when they are curious about the outcome of the research, when confidentiality is ensured and when they feel they are being treated as a genuinely valid source of input (see my previous comments about co-operation and reciprocity between the researcher and the participants, and also my points on ethics below). Individuals are also more likely to participate when the research has social relevance and revolves around existing community and social relationships. If all the above elements are in place, you can then also consider whether to offer monetary incentives as a way of ensuring attendance and showing your appreciation to participants.

Once you have identified participants with the requisite characteristics of your target audience, you will have to write to them personally or call to invite them to the meeting. It is important that when you approach people individually, they feel that you sincerely request and appreciate their involvement and ideas. It is a good idea not to use the term 'focus group' either when contacting potential participants or during the actual session, as the use of terminology often alienates people and may affect the spontaneity of contributions. Instead, you can invite participants to 'discuss' or 'share ideas with others', thus signalling that the discussion will be informal (Krueger 1994).

One other question worth thinking about is how much to say about the research when inviting people to attend. As it is important not to lead the participants and to have their individual, unrehearsed opinions, it is wise at this stage to provide only general information about the study and its anticipated benefits. Details about the goals and design of the study and specific answers to questions can be best provided at the end of the focus group session. You may also want to be careful about sharing information on other specific aspects of the research. For example, I made the conscious decision not to mention before the session that I was interested in the 'language' of my participants, as I wanted the focus *for them* to be on what they would say, and not on how they would say it. Although the focus *for me* as the researcher was not primarily on the participants' attitudes or opinions on the topic of marriage, but rather on the linguistic practices and repertoires that they brought to their arguments, it was more appropriate, more immediate and less vague to ask the participants to focus on their views on the topic.

After individuals have agreed to take part, you should send them a personalized follow-up invitation with details of the date, time and venue for the meeting, a brief proposed agenda, and your contact details. Efforts should be made to ensure that the time and place are convenient for the participants (more on this later). The importance of attendance and of participants' input should be emphasized in the follow-up invitation, and again, one or two days before the session, when you call people to remind them to attend. You need also to have a reserve list of participants who have agreed to attend at short notice if necessary. This is because, in many cases, some of the participants who originally agreed to take part will not attend for various reasons (for example, illness, forgetfulness, hectic schedule or traffic delays).

The role of the moderator

Although it may appear to outsiders to be relatively passive, the role of the moderator or group facilitator is absolutely critical. First, you will need to decide if you, as the researcher, will be the best person to moderate the focus groups. This decision will depend on a number of factors:

The topic and composition of the focus groups

It is important that the moderator understands not only the topic, but also the culture and traditions of the focus group participants, as for example in sessions with particular ethnic or racial groups. The moderator should have some understanding of the community or communities researched, in some cases through having been in contact with them in the past. Other considerations are the moderator's gender, age, race, socio-economic and professional status. For example, a man will not be the best person to interview women on the topic of domestic violence, and it is not appropriate for a lecturer to moderate a group consisting of her students. As discussed above, a perceived or actual power difference between the moderator and the participants can be detrimental to the quality of the focus group discussion.

Methodological factors

It is preferable to have the same moderator for the whole series of focus groups, unless someone of a different age or sex is more appropriate for one or more of the sessions. One reason is that having the same moderator for all groups will reduce the problem of different styles, which can make the analysis of the data more difficult. Such differences in style are also important to consider when, occasionally, two moderators are involved in facilitating one focus group; in this case, it is better if one moderator facilitates and directs the discussion, while the other takes notes, observes the discussion and checks the recording equipment. Another reason for having one moderator for all groups is that consistency of moderating can help reduce the risk of manipulation and bias. Krueger (1994) notes that in order to avoid manipulation, it is the researcher, rather than other individuals or groups, who should have control over the critical aspects of the study: participant selection, question development, moderation and analysis. The researcher also acting as moderator may help increase coherence across the stages of the methodology, minimize the conflict between methodological assumptions and styles, and limit the possibility of intervention and manipulation (for example, by clients or the organization benefiting from the research). But these benefits are also possible when the other conditions discussed here are met: the topic and group composition are suitable (previous point), and the moderator has skill and experience (next point).

The skills required of a good moderator

This is by far the most important factor to consider before deciding who should moderate the group discussions. Ideally, the moderator should have some familiarity with moderating focus groups, <u>particularly with probing, open-ended questioning, focused discussion and group dynamics</u>. Apart from some experience, however, it is even more important that the moderator has an affinity for the task, the ability to <u>listen sincerely</u> and to <u>inspire people to talk</u>. She or he should be able to make the necessary transitions from one topic or issue to the next, <u>while maintaining group enthusiasm and interest for the topic,</u> and having a curiosity and respect for the participants (Krueger 1994). The degree of structure, control and direction adopted by moderators will depend on the goals of the research, the type of data that needs to be obtained and the moderator's preferred style, but generally speaking, a moderator should be aware of the following:

1 A good moderator has *good personal, interpersonal, communication and managing skills.* Above all, a good moderator is a *good listener:* in the best focus groups, people talk to each other, not to the moderator.
2 A good moderator appears '*neutral*', *opinion-free and non-judgemental.* This means encouraging both positive and negative comments, being careful not to communicate approval or disapproval (including through body language) and withholding personal opinion, in order not to favour or influence participants towards a position.
3 A good moderator is *confident and in control* (i.e. keeps the discussion relevant), while at the same time being *flexible and adaptable* to the ways in which the discussion progresses and develops.

These qualities are crucial for a successful focus group, as they will promote the participants' trust in the moderator and increase the likelihood of open, interactive dialogue. They also contribute to minimizing the risk of bias that can result from the moderator leading the participants or the participants responding to the moderator's pre-judices.

Now let us look at the demanding role of the moderator in some detail. If the researcher and the moderator are the same person – as it is likely to be the case in many small-scale projects in the social sciences – moderating the focus group is one more responsibility for the researcher, in addition to clarifying, planning and conducting the research, recruiting participants, interpreting and analysing the data and publishing the results. As a moderator, you will be involved in planning, hosting and conducting the focus group, but you may also take responsibility for managing the project resources, setting up the room and the appropriate equipment for the session, and timing and recording the group discussions.
More specifically, the role of the moderator during a focus group session is to:

Maintain the group's focus and keep the discussion on track

This involves ensuring that the key questions (see Section 4) are discussed, that the discussion is moving on, that participants do not shift away from the topic or dominate the discussion, and that all group participants contribute and get the chance to speak. The moderator must observe and at the same time manage the group dynamics, as these revolve around the participants' comments, questions and positive or negative reactions. Depending on the aims of the research, moderating the focus group can be more or less directive. Non-directive moderators may concentrate on allowing the discussion to flow naturally, as long as it remains on the topic. Non-directive approaches are more appropriate when the purpose of the focus group is to generate new ideas, while more directive and structured approaches may suit groups where the aim is to generate hypotheses, explore problems, or deal with sensitive topics. Good moderators know that the amount of direction will influence the types and quality of the data obtained (Stewart and Shamdasani 1990), and are prepared to be flexible in directing the focus group discussion.

Guide, stimulate and facilitate the discussion

The moderator achieves this via a number of pre-determined, clear and carefully developed open-ended questions, and through the use of probes (these are discussed in detail in Section 4). Remember that a moderator does not interview people, hold a position of power or influence, or inhibit the flow of ideas by intervening. The moderator promotes debate and interaction among participants, and at certain points may challenge participants or draw out their differences, to tease out a diverse range of meanings on the topic under discussion (Gibbs 1997). Again, the moderator's guiding and facilitating style will depend on the group objectives. To encourage the exchange of new ideas, the moderator may assume a role similar to any of the participants, where discussants feed off each other in an open and creative manner. On the other hand, to encourage the group to focus on specific issues or problems, the moderator may play a more leading, central role in the communication exchange.

Put participants at ease

This involves providing clear explanations of the purpose of the group, assuring participants that there are no right or wrong answers, and encouraging them to share their views (including controversial or radically different opinions from the rest of the group). It also involves establishing rapport and an informal, warm and friendly atmosphere. To achieve this, the moderator needs to be insightful, empathetic, patient, open to other people's views and genuinely interested in their contributions. A good sense of humour can also be an asset here. Sometimes, when the research is being conducted for an organization, it will be necessary to assure people that the moderator does not work for that organization and is not accountable to them. To put participants at ease, anonymity and confidentiality must also be guaranteed, and the actions taken to achieve these must be stated clearly and in no misleading terms.

To summarize, the moderator will use her or his skills (as described earlier) to maintain the focus of the discussion, to guide, stimulate and facilitate the discussion, and to put participants at ease by creating an atmosphere of openness and interaction. It is a complex and challenging role.

> the focus group [...] should be [...] focused yet casual, moderated by the researcher who guides but does not lead, controls but does not inhibit the conversation, and who (among other things) ensures everyone has equal opportunity to express their natural [sic] vocabulary: in short, the researcher is a perfect combination of understanding empathy and disciplined detachment, while the respondents are orderly, natural, inter-

active, and utterly self revealing. In other words, impossible.   (Barker and Brooks 1998, 24)

The task is not impossible, however. If we take as given the fact that there is no typical focus group, and that you will always be learning new things as a researcher from one group to the next, there are certain things to pay attention to and to avoid when moderating focus groups. Silverman (2000) proposes paying attention to the subtle differences in participant responses, making informed predictions about what may and may not work, and thinking about various possible scenarios of the discussion. Importantly, a good moderator understands the background to the research, the problems, the difficulties and internal political issues facing a group, and the different types of participants; does not take verbalizations at face value, but probes deeply and challenges participants through a variety of methods, in order to get behind people's defences and rationalizations; identifies what is established, interprets what has been heard, verifies and confirms what has been said and identifies patterns within and between groups; and modifies the discussion guide, even in the middle of groups, to pursue new ideas and follow hunches and, when appropriate, takes the research beyond the original objectives (Silverman 2000).

Many researchers may be discouraged from moderating focus groups on the basis of this list! In my own experience with conducting as well as participating in focus groups, one most important element assumed in the list above is that the moderator should be know-ledgeable about and comfortable with different styles of interviewing: flexible enough to switch from directive to non-directive approaches as the discussion unfolds. The directive approach, which can allow for greater and more detailed coverage of topics, should complement a non-directive approach, which can allow for greater group interaction, synergy, spontaneity and the discovery of ideas (Stewart and Shamdasani 1990). The difficulty lies in identifying when one or the other approach is necessary and likely to produce the best results. You need to be considerably alert, and this means that you should not assume that the moderating is going well just on the basis of how you sound or how the group seems to be going. Again, Silverman (2000) points out that a focus group may appear to be working well, with participants interacting in a lively manner and the moderator probing and getting answers successfully, while in reality the exchange of rationalizations and other defensive communications may be taking place. Defences, such as projection, evasion or distortion, are typically used by people to protect themselves from feeling embarrassed, ignored, rejected or unimportant (ibid.). In Sections 4 and 5 you will find information on ways of anticipating such defences, and a variety of techniques which can be used to verify and challenge what people say and to encourage different perspectives.

After reading this section, you should have enough information to decide whether you, the researcher, or someone else would make a good moderator. I proceed in this book on the assumption that the researcher also moderates the focus groups. If you wish to find out about procedures for recruiting a moderator, see Chapter 13 in Krueger (1994) for some guidelines.

Selecting a location and other practicalities of setting up focus groups

Focus groups have been conducted in various locations, such as people's homes, restaurants, bars, hotels, public buildings and rented facilities. Although it is very important to have a relaxed informal environment, you should bear in mind that bars and restaurants can be noisy; music, other people and food and drink instruments can seriously interfere with the tape recording of the session. Selecting a location is as important as finding the right venue. It is best to choose a central location that is easy to find, and that would not be too far for the participants to travel. The room for the focus group session should be light and airy, and ideally free of visual or other distractions, such as noise or traffic.

Your participants will feel more comfortable in some places than in others. Ask yourself these questions: what is the place and time where these participants are likely to talk? Does the place and time make a difference on who is entitled to ask questions, and in what manner or protocol? If the participants are a pre-existing group, it may be a good idea to have the meeting where they regularly meet, although, to take two examples, employees may not feel happy to ask or answer questions in the workplace, and some Muslim women may not feel comfortable talking in a public place. For most projects, neutral locations are best, in order to avoid negative or positive associations with a particular site or building (Powell and Single 1996).

For the actual session, it is usually best if participants are seated around an oval table, together with the moderator, to ensure eye contact for all and an atmosphere of equality and informality. Some research suggests placing the least talkative participants directly across from the moderator and the most talkative off to the sides of the table (Wells 1974), but this will only be possible if the moderator knows about people's personalities before the meeting. As a moderator, you need to have a diagram with the participants' names and seating arrangement. It is useful to provide name tags for the members of the group, using only first names. This has a practical function, in ensuring that everyone is able to address everyone else, but also helps create a more friendly, informal atmosphere. Also provide refreshments, and lunch, if the session is held over lunch – a time when many participants are available for attending a focus group.

You need to plan recording the session with either an audio or audio-video recorder, and secure the right equipment. Tape recording is of course very important for the purposes of transcription and analysis, and it would be better to use equipment that allows for high-quality recording. Because of the number of people involved in a focus group discussion, it is often difficult to get high-quality recording and to identify who is speaking at any given time. Good recording equipment, as well as an assistant's or observer's notes, are two resources that can help in that direction.

It is better to use more than one audio-recorder and more than one microphone, in order to capture what is said across the table. Use portable but robust recorders, with internal and extension microphones, that can be both mains and battery operated. Make sure you have enough tapes and spare batteries for the session, and back up copies after the session. The recorders and microphones should be visible but not in the way; normally, two or three small recorders/microphones placed at the centre and sides of the table, and as far away from background noises as possible, are more than adequate for picking up the conversation. Always check that the equipment is set and that it works before the session. It is a good idea not to switch off the recorders at the end of the session as, in my experience, participants almost always make important points after the end of the discussion!

Video recording is recommended by some researchers, particularly if the research project has an interest in group interaction. But Krueger (1994) sees videotaping as obtrusive, affecting participant spontaneity, and usually not worth the considerable effort of arranging the equipment and of having several cameras and camera operators. Nevertheless, videotaping may be necessary for some focus groups, in which case every effort should be made not to distract the participants and to keep the operators' presence discreet. I suggest that if you think that the quality of the discussion is more important than the facilities and technological devices used, then you can rely on audio-recording and fieldnotes to capture and analyse the focus group discussions. Fieldnotes can be anything from scratchnotes, diagrams and lists, to narrative accounts of talk and notes about non-verbal communication. They are usually taken during the session by an assistant or observer who has good knowledge of the aims of the research project, and they will be invaluable for the analysis stage.

Market researchers tend also to use one-way mirrors for their focus groups, so that their clients can listen to the proceedings and observe the participants' body language. In those studies, the presence of a mirror is sometimes mentioned to the participants, and sometimes not. I believe that one-way mirrors can be obtrusive if participants are aware of their existence, and they raise serious ethical problems, especially when the procedures are secretive. However, your decision about whether to use these will depend on your objectives and methodological assumptions. For example, many social research projects prioritize ethnographic over experimental approaches, and some of their inherent assumptions about the researcher and those researched would be in conflict with the use of mirrors for observation purposes – for instance, doubting the existence of a 'neutral self', and locating yourself, as a researcher, within the research topic rather than outside it.

Finally, one or two practical tips that can greatly help with your planning. It is best to make a written plan of the focus group, which will make your research design concrete and at the same time develop your thinking about the research. The plan should include details of scheduling, the chronological sequence, the questions to be asked (with timings – see 'topic guide' in Section 4) and the costs involved. You should expect aspects of the plan to change during the session, particularly the order and timings of the questions, but you should cover all the questions or topics planned. I also find it helpful to write down the agenda for the meeting: welcoming the participants, reviewing the goal and rules of the meeting, introductions, questions and answers, closing (see Section 5 on conducting focus groups).

Ethical issues

Research ethics is about the moral values and principles which guide and underpin the research process. As in other methods of social research, you will need to make some important ethical decisions during the planning of your focus groups. These range from the more obvious decisions, such as the use of one-way mirrors and confidentiality, to more subtle issues, such as offering cash incentives for people to attend.

First, during the early stages of recruiting participants, you will have to decide how much to tell them about the research. There are obviously no guidelines for this, and a lot will depend on the nature and topic of the research project. Try to be honest and truthful in what you do tell participants. It is good practice before the session to inform people about the purpose of the research (in general terms) and the future uses of their contributions, and during the session to keep them informed about the expectations of the group (Gibbs 1997). These expectations will generally be that participants are free to talk, not pressurized to speak or to speak in a specific way, not expected to reach consensus or to provide answers, and that they can decide what and how much to disclose to the group. Tell participants that they are being recorded, unless you have decided to ask for their permission first in the letter you sent them. I would also suggest that you tell them they are being observed, and introduce the observers who will be in the same room during the discussion.

A particular issue to consider in focus group research is confidentiality. It is difficult to assure participants of this, when what they say is shared with others in the group and with the moderator. Anonymity is possible through the use of pseudonyms, although these do not always work, as certain details in the transcripts can sometimes give away information about the place and people involved. It is important to ensure confidentiality as much as possible, particularly if the topic is sensitive. The researcher is responsible for keeping the data anonymous and for analysing and publishing the data in ways that respect confidentiality, for example, by not attributing quotations to specific speakers. Participants in a focus group are also responsible for keeping confidential what they hear during the discussion, and the moderator should encourage them to do so.

The research process involves ethical questions that revolve around issues of power. Consider the power relations between the moderator and the participants; between the researcher who publishes the results of a focus group and the participants; between an organization involved in the research process and the researcher; and among the focus group participants themselves. Ask yourself about the effect of including more powerful and less powerful people in the same focus group and/or from the same environment. Also, how can you address the possibility of participants perceiving the researcher or moderator as someone in a privileged position, i.e. a decision-maker or 'expert'? Perhaps a small, visible way in which you can minimize such an impression is by offering incentives other than cash to participants. In fact, offering a cash incentive for focus group attendance can raise other ethical issues too – for example, does this practice make it more difficult for those researchers who cannot afford to pay respondents?

Summary

This section has aimed to help you with planning and organizing focus groups for research. It has discussed the use of pilot focus groups, decisions in selecting the participants, the role of the moderator and other practical and ethical issues. Some salient points were made:

- To plan your focus groups, you need to be clear about the research aims and purposes, the topic or issue to be discussed and the anticipated outcomes.
- A pilot focus group is important for your planning, as it will give information on the likely themes for discussion and people's responses to them, and on the dynamics and mechanics of the group discussion.
- Commonality and heterogeneity of focus group participants, in terms of demographic characteristics and their familiarity with the topic, will depend on the research question(s).
- You need to be extremely aware of subtle perceived differences and power relations within a group.
- Whether the researcher also moderates the focus groups will depend on the topic and composition of the groups, on specific methodological factors and, more importantly, on the skills required of a good moderator.
- A good moderator has good personal, interpersonal, communication and managing skills, is a good and

non-judgemental listener, and is confident and flexible at the same time.

- The moderator's role is to maintain the focus of the discussion, to guide, stimulate and facilitate the discussion, and to put participants at ease by creating an atmosphere of openness and interaction.
- Informal environments, neutral locations and good quality and non-intrusive recording equipment work best for focus groups.
- It is important to try to be as ethical and as honest as possible in your research.

4

Developing and Asking Questions

This section offers an introduction to developing your topic guide or questioning route for a focus group, and looks at the different types and kinds of questions that can be used during a session. It examines how you can use these different types and kinds of questions to get to different aspects of the topic and achieve different results.

The topic guide or questioning route

Questions in focus groups appear to be deceptively simple, spontaneous and unstructured, but in reality they are carefully predetermined, sequenced and purposefully open-ended. The researcher has developed a *questioning route* or a *topic guide*, which is planned to generate a broad yet focused, in-depth discussion on the context and various components of the topic. The moderator will usually follow this pre-planned script of questions and topics, in more or less structured ways, in order to achieve specific goals during the session, i.e. to obtain specific information.

The topic guide is a list of topics or issues to be explored during the session, containing words or phrases that remind the moderator of each topic, while the questioning route is a sequence of questions in complete sentences (Krueger 1994). The topic guide links the questions to wider contexts and frameworks by generating discussion: it does not have a question and answer format. It may often appear more spontaneous than a questioning route, because the moderator will typically incorporate the participants' own words into the question. It is worth remembering, however, that this adaptability presupposes a skilled moderator, who in this case can spontaneously phrase the topic 'into a coherent, single-dimension question' (Krueger 1994, p.54) such as, 'How has this distance education programme changed your professional life?'

To develop a topic guide, you first need to clarify the research questions of the project, and brainstorm a number of key topics/questions, before drafting a question order with timings. You should aim to have around ten focused questions, and fewer if the topic is complex or emotional or if the group is considerably diverse and heterogeneous. The guide should be clear, non-academic, and understandable to the participants. In addition to headings of topics and questions, it usually includes approximate timings for each topic (about 15 minutes), and prompts (discussed later in this section). Depending on the focus group, it may also include presentations or demonstrations and *stimulus materials*. Stimulus materials are often used to introduce foreign or controversial concepts, or encourage interaction and creativity among the participants, and can be anything from a flip-chart, magazines or tape recordings, to abstract art.

This is an example of a broad topic guide for focus groups on the topic of marriage (Litosseliti 1999). The timings and prompts used are not included here.

- *Asking participants to introduce themselves: their name/where they come from/where they live*
- *Unpacking the concept of marriage/Getting to different interpretations*

  What does marriage mean to you?/Does it concern you?

  Is there a difference between ...?/What is the difference...?

  How do different people look at different forms of marriage?

  Advantages and disadvantages of marriage

  Advantages and disadvantages of cohabitation
- *Identifying and describing change*

  Change in the way we think about marriage as an institution (in the UK)

  Change in the way we think about cohabiting couples (in the UK)

  Links to particular social changes and how they affect people

  Change of gender roles and relations
- *Exploring the arguments in the marriage-cohabitation debate*

  Arguments by different social groups/Moral arguments

  Arguments involving gender/Moral arguments

  Arguments about family relationships and children/ Moral arguments
- *Personal experiences of marriage and cohabitation*

  Parents and other influences on the topic

  People's own domestic arrangements and decisions on the topic
- *Examining specific arguments within a newspaper debate (between two participants) about marriage and co-habitation (in the UK)*
- *Summary of ideas discussed/Reflection/Additional comments/ Conclusion*

In your topic guide, you can incorporate other media, such as images or advertisements. For example, the topic guide in the 'Global Citizenship and the Environment' project (Myers, Szerszynski and Urry 1996–99) used clips of advertisements as prompts in the first focus group, and still images and clips from documentaries in the second focus group with the same participants. In between focus groups, participants were asked to find their own examples of 'global citizenship' to discuss with the group, which meant that participants were also involved in shaping the topic guide for the next session.

Whether you use a topic guide or a questioning route, you will have to reflect upon and carefully develop the appropriate questions to be raised during the focus group: 'quality answers are directly related to quality questions' (Krueger 1994, p.53). Start with brainstorming any questions that are relevant to the topic, then work on refining and sequencing them. At this stage, it is quite useful to do this kind of brainstorming and refining together with other interested parties, such as co-researchers, the moderator (if different), decision-makers and people in organizations involved in the research. In order to refine and sequence the questions, identify which are the general questions for all groups, which are specific questions for each group and which are the critical questions for all groups. Bear in mind that there will be a lot of revisions of the questioning route and also some new questions arising during the session, therefore you should allow for flexibility in your planning. Such revisions are accommodated in the 'rolling interview guide', often used for a series of focus groups (Stewart and Shamdasani 1990). This involves developing a revised guide for each subsequent focus group on the basis of the outcome of the preceding group. You will have to weigh the advantages of this approach against the disadvantages, particularly the difficulty in ending up comparing groups where different topic guides were used.

Types of questions

It is important to sequence your questions. The initial goal during the session is to get participants relaxed and involved in the discussion, therefore at the beginning it is better to ask simple and factual questions, rather than complex or controversial ones. It takes time for participants to warm up and feel comfortable about disclosing and responding to information. It is also easier for them to talk about the present first, and then about the past or the future.

When developing the interview guide, you should make sure that there is a progression from the more general, unstructured questions to the more specific, cued ones (the funnel approach). At the beginning of your guide it is useful to have uncued questions such as, 'Tell me about ...', while presenting specific ideas and alternatives later via cued questions. In general, uncued questions are good for introducing topics or new aspects of a topic, and are typically open-ended (discussed further below). Cued, specific questions solicit participants' reactions and attitudes, and so they tend to move the discussion in particular directions. Such questions are especially useful when participants are uncertain about specific ideas that have been shared, and when the moderator wishes to probe in more detail.

In addition, the most important questions should be near the top of the guide, while the less significant ones should be near the end (Stewart and Shamdasani 1990). This ordering implies a linear coverage of each topic, from the general to the specific, before moving to the next topic in order of importance. However, it is unlikely in practice that group interaction will develop in a linear way, and most of the time there will be a lot of overlap and cause and effect links between topics. It is a good idea, therefore, to consider the general-to-specific and more-to-least-important rules as guidelines, while at the same time remaining alert to the different ways in which your guide may be adapted. It must be quite obvious by now why a skilled, knowledgeable and flexible moderator is so crucial.

Krueger identifies the following specific types of questions: an *opening question, introductory questions, key questions, transition questions,* and *ending questions* (1994). The opening question is usually a factual question that can be answered by everyone quickly. Typical opening questions (see also Section 5 following) could be:

- 'What is your name and what are you studying?'
- 'Tell us your name and what you like doing.'

Factual questions in general are useful for ice-breaking and putting participants at ease, as they involve no risk-taking. Similarly, when used appropriately in the course of a discussion, they can be useful 'for neutralising emotionally charged groups or discussions' (Stewart and Shamdasani 1990, p.83).

Introductory questions introduce the general topic of discussion and aim to foster discussion and interaction (Krueger 1994). For example:

- 'What is the most serious problem in your neighbour-hood?'
- 'Do you enjoy reading fiction?'
- 'What do you think about marriage?'

These are the types of questions that gradually lead into the key questions. The key questions correspond to the main research questions of your study, that is, they are directly related to the purpose of the focus group. The key questions are planned in advance of the focus group and are clearly indicated in your topic guide; they are the most important ones to discuss and develop during the session, and the ones to analyse in detail after the session.

Throughout the discussion, the moderator will also ask what Krueger calls transition questions. As with all inter-action, these are important discursive mechanisms, used for a variety of purposes (see also Section 5): to clarify a point, to move the discussion onto another topic, to test a concept, to steer the group back to a key question, or to encourage a broader view of the topic. For example:

- 'Could you say more about...?'
- 'Can you try to think of any alternatives?'
- 'We've been talking about ... Could we now move on to...?'

Finally, the ending questions of the focus group allow participants to provide additional information, to talk about their impressions of the focus group, and to close the discussion. According to Krueger, these questions are important for the analysis, because they allow reflection. The most common ending questions ask participants to consider a summary of key points from the discussion, or to identify the most important aspects of the topic. For example, the moderator will undertake to summarize the key questions and ideas that emerged from the discus-sion, and then ask:

- *'Is this an adequate summary?'*

The answer to this question will be important for analysis, as it gives participants the opportunity to reflect upon the discussion and clarify or expand on what they consider to be the key ideas on the topic.

The 'all things considered' question has a similar function, and is as important for analysis. This is a ques-tion asking participants to identify the most important aspect or factor in relation to the topic, such as:

- *'Of all the . . . that were discussed, which one is most important to you?'*

Krueger rightly recommends that, instead of assuming during the analysis that what is mentioned frequently during the discussion is of greater importance, the researcher should include a specific question to allow participants to articulate what *they* see as most important (1994).

Finally, about ten minutes before the end of a focus group, the moderator may give a very short overview of the purpose of the study, and ask one final question:

- *'Have we missed anything?'*

I would now like to turn to the kinds of questions a moderator may be asking, and to the different data we can obtain by using specific kinds of questions and avoiding others.

Kinds of questions

Apart from background/demographic questions, an interviewer can ask people questions about *behaviours*, i.e. what they have done or are doing, *opinions/ values*, i.e. what they think about a topic, *feelings, knowledge* about a topic, and *sensory* questions about what people have seen, heard and so on (Patton 1990). This gives a very general idea about the kinds of questions you could be asking. But what is crucial in the focus group situation is knowing what sort of responses certain kinds of questions are likely to elicit, and the possible ways in which the manner of asking certain questions can affect the content, process and direction of the discussion. An obvious example is that responses will vary if a question is asked in terms of the past, present or future. You will also get different responses, for example, unanticipated comments, if you ask a question in an open-ended manner, rather than asking a closed question, where cues are provided by the moderator. Let us look at possible kinds of questions you should aim to use in a focus group, and questions to avoid.

Use open-ended questions

Open-ended questions are broader and allow people considerable freedom to choose what to say, how much, and how to say it, while closed questions tend to limit participants' answer options (Stewart and Shamdasani 1990). Examples of open-ended questions would be:

- 'What do you think of [a particular event, place, decision, concept]?'
- 'What do you like best about...?'
- 'How did you feel about...?'
- 'Where do you go when...?'

The rationale behind such questions is that they are not leading the respondents; the response is not implied by the question. There are times when leading questions are useful in the moderating process: usually later on in the discussion, and particularly if your intention is to probe into a sensitive topic, get participants to choose one answer over another or to get beyond surface responses. But to avoid bias, where participants simply respond to a question without generating their own ideas, such questions should be used sparingly, even if, from a practical point of view, they may be easier to analyse compared to open-ended questions (Stewart and Shamdasani 1990).

Avoid yes/no questions

Dichotomous questions that invite the respondents to answer with a 'yes' or 'no' are effectively closed questions.

In addition to limiting the respondents' answer options, they can stifle group discussion, and lead to polarizing opinions.

Use neutral questions

In line with what was said above, the use of neutral questions can help to minimize the bias resulting from leading the participants, and can also safeguard against the value judgements sometimes made by inexperienced moderators. Generally speaking, the use of 'loaded', judgmental or evocative wording should be avoided, as it can put respondents in a reactive or defensive mode. Krueger also recommends against questions that contain words such as 'satisfied', 'to what extent', and 'how much', especially early on in the interview (1994). For example, it will be more productive to ask:

- 'What did you think of the anti-drug campaign at your school?'
- 'In what ways did the campaign make a difference?'

rather than:

- 'Were you satisfied with the outcomes of the campaign?'
- 'Did you support the campaign?'

The latter questions will be helpful for getting to deeper meaning in the discussion and for probing as the talk becomes more specific. It is useful to formulate such questions by using the things the participants actually say – in the example above, the words a participant has used to express satisfaction with or support for the particular campaign.

Avoid 'why' questions

Krueger points out that asking 'why' invites participants to give quick answers that seem rational and appropriate. 'Why' questions also invite justification, which can cause defensiveness and inhibit people's responses. Further, this kind of question often assumes a cause-and-effect relationship that actually may not exist, and thus can be confusing or misleading (1994). If you use 'why' questions, you should be specific (for example, 'Why did you decide to take part in the campaign?'), or break the question down into different questions (Krueger 1994). For example:

- 'What influenced your decision to take part in the campaign?'
- 'What aspects of your role in the campaign did you particularly like?'

Another alternative to asking a 'why' question is to ask a 'feel' question:

- 'How do you feel about being involved in this campaign?'

'Feel' questions ask participants to share their personal feelings, and this often represents a risk. Stewart and Shamdasani (1990) describe these as the most dangerous and most fertile questions. As a moderator, you can make the best of responses to such questions by extending them to other group participants and linking them to the key ideas shared. For example:

- 'What would it feel like for someone at the opposite end of this campaign?'

Use clear questions

This means non-lengthy questions, questions with one dimension, and questions that are understandable to participants, free of jargon and technical terms (Krueger 1994). It is difficult to understand as well as respond to unclear questions, and careful planning of your interview guide in advance should ensure that unclear questions are not asked. It is a good exercise to identify and separate the many dimensions of a question during the planning stage. For example, asking whether a particular campaign has been useful, suitable and effective would be a multi-part question, which can better be phrased as three questions. Equally, you need to be aware of the multiple meanings of words: the description of something as 'effective' may be understood differently by different individuals.

Use focused questions

As already discussed, to focus the discussion you need to move from more general to more specific questions. Focused questions are presented in a context, and therefore it is important that participants know enough, through general questions, about the context surrounding specific critical questions (Krueger 1994).

Use lots of probing

Probes are asking participants to provide more information, and to expand on or clarify their comments. Typical examples are, 'Could you explain further ...?', 'How do you mean this ...?', 'I think you're saying ...', 'Do you mean ...?', 'What else ...?', 'There may be a relationship between …', 'What do other people think about ..?' Silence or pauses and minimal responses such as 'Mmm', 'Huh', 'Yes', can also be very useful, when appropriately used. Probing is more effective and less threatening for the participants, compared to asking people directly to express views, or their agreement and disagreement on a topic. I discuss probes in detail and with additional examples in the next section of the book.

Summary

This section has shown how different types and kinds of questions can be used in focus groups to get to different aspects of the topic and achieve different results. In particular:

- Focus group questions are carefully developed, refined and sequenced in order to generate focused in-depth discussion.
- A topic guide or questioning route is essential, and may include topics, questions, timings, prompts and stimulus materials.
- In general, simple, factual, general, unstructured and important questions come before complex, controversial, specific, cued and less significant ones.
- Opening, introductory, key, transition and ending questions are typically used in group discussions.
- It is preferable to use open-ended and neutral questions rather than closed or 'loaded' ones, and to avoid 'yes/no' and 'why' questions. Questions should also be clear and focused, complemented by probing.

5

Conducting Focus Groups

This section deals with conducting a focus group, including preparation immediately before the session and following up a discussion. The different stages of a focus group session are described and the process of moderating is illustrated with examples of an introduction, different questions, methods and discursive strategies.

Before the focus group session

Assuming that you are both researcher and moderator of the focus groups you will be conducting, by this stage you will have recruited the participants, reminded them to attend one or two days before the actual session, and secured the appropriate location and equipment. You will have carefully prepared the discussion topic guide or questioning route and have a written plan of the session.

You may have planned the various stages of the session together with an assistant moderator. Co-operation between the two moderators is necessary, so that roles and responsibilities are understood and agreed upon before the session. The moderator guides and facilitates the discussion, while the assistant moderator takes detailed notes, operates the equipment and makes sure the participants are comfortable. The assistant moderator's notes will provide valuable information on certain revealing or eloquently expressed comments and on participants' para-linguistic behaviour: gestures, posture, laughs and so on. These notes will facilitate the transcription of the discussion (for instance, by providing a seating plan and by linking a quote to a speaker) and will greatly aid the analysis. The assistant may also be involved in writing questions, comments or summaries on a flip-chart during the discussion, and is well placed to draw attention to additional or missing points towards the end of the session.

I prefer to keep the outsiders present in a group to a minimum, and have found it possible (especially with small groups) to do without an assistant, but with the invaluable help of an observer. The observer is a person with some knowledge of the aims of the research who attends and observes the discussion but does not take part in it – and unlike an assistant moderator, is not responsible for the equipment or involved in supporting the moderator during the session. For my focus group work in the past, I have relied on the help of colleagues who were social scientists with an interest in communication, discourse and group dynamics, and who agreed to act as observers. The observer should be introduced to the group at the very beginning of the discussion. As the moderator, you should explicitly tell the group that the observer is there to listen and to take notes that can facilitate the research process, not to judge or assess what will be discussed. In my groups, I asked the observer to take notes which we then discussed after the end of the session. The observer's insight was crucial for a better understanding and analysis of the issues raised during the session, and for pointing out things I had missed.

On the day of the session, it is always a good idea to arrive early, in order to set up and check the equipment, make changes in the room, place the name tags, make arrangements for refreshments and/or food, and have materials and handouts ready (if appropriate). You should welcome participants individually as they arrive and ensure they are comfortable. The atmosphere, especially during the critical first moments of the focus group, should be as friendly, open and informal as possible. It is preferable to have food and refreshments before settling down to begin the session.

Stages of the focus group session

As the moderator, you will begin by welcoming and thanking the participants and offering an introduction. Talk briefly about who you are and what your role is, the research project in general, the topic and purpose of the discussion, and why the particular individuals were selected to attend. At this early stage, you should also indicate how long the discussion will last (it should not take longer than you say it will), talk a bit about the format of the interview, and set the ground rules (for example, you may want to encourage participants either to ask questions during the session or wait until the end of the session). You will want to clarify important rules and responsibilities from the beginning. It may be a good idea to write these on a flip-chart, so that they are visible throughout the session:

> *You should speak freely*
> *Your opinions are important*
> *There are no right and wrong answers, we are interested in both positive and negative comments*
> *Don't worry about building consensus*
> *Don't worry about being on the right track*
> *Please don't talk at the same time; allow others to speak*

This is also the time to draw attention to recording and explain the reasons for recording the discussion – namely that this ensures the researcher does not miss any of the comments and opinions. As discussed earlier, it is important to assure participants that their contributions will be anonymous and confidential. This involves explaining that people's names will be changed on reports and other publications, and indicating who will get access to their answers, and possibly how their answers will be analysed.

Here is an example of an introduction from Litosseliti (1999).

Example of a focus group introduction

Welcome and thank you for taking the time to attend our focus group.

The purpose of this meeting is to discuss your ideas, opinions and experiences on the topic of marriage. What you discuss here today will be very helpful for my individual research project in this area, and after today's session you are welcome to ask me questions about the research and about our discussion.

You have all been invited because you have some things in common (for example, you have been married) and because you are likely to have a variety of important views and experiences to share about this topic.

The idea of the group discussion is to allow you to share your views in a relaxed and informal environment. There are no right or wrong answers, but rather different points of view. All points of view, and both positive and negative comments, are important. Of course, what to say, how to say it, and how much to say is up to you. You should not worry about what you are expected to say, whether you are on the right track, or whether you should reach consensus. But please make sure that you allow others to speak, you do not talk at the same time, and do not interrupt others.

So that I do not miss any of your comments, I would like

71

to tape record our discussion. I have asked for your permission to do this, as it will make my research work much easier. I should point out that your contributions will be anonymous and confidential, and that any published research will contain changed names.

Our discussion will last about one hour and a half. During that time, I would like to explore a number of issues on this topic and hear everyone's responses. It would be better to keep your questions about this research project until the end, but please feel free to ask questions relating to the topic throughout the discussion.

I would like to start by asking you to introduce yourselves to everyone, by telling us your name, where you live, and where you come from.

This is the *forming stage* of the group discussion (Tuckman 1965; Tuckman and Jensen 1977; McNamara 1999), where participants do not know each other and do not feel part of the group yet, but are gathering impressions about others; here we get formalities and politeness, rather than trust among group members. Participants rely on safe and simple patterns of behaviour, while it is the responsibility of the moderator to do the talking and provide guidance and direction. The emphasis is on introducing the task, and defining the scope of the task, approaches to it, and related rules. It is crucial at this stage that the moderator creates a relaxed and friendly atmosphere, brings energy to the session, and avoids controversial or serious topics.

As mentioned before, focus groups are unpredictable events: one group may be relaxed, interesting and free-flowing, while another may be dull, reserved and cautious. It is expected that at the initial stage of a group session there will be some awkwardness and anxiety, as participants are wondering about the nature and achievements of the session, what will be asked of them, whether they will be liked and accepted by the group, and what risks or pressures they may have to face. People normally have concerns and fears about sounding dull or stupid, saying embarrassing things, saying too little or too much, being nervous and so on (McNamara 1999). Also remember that the discussion of the topics of interest for the researcher may not feel natural to the participants (Morgan and Krueger 1997). It is therefore understandable that participants are likely to focus, at this initial stage, on safe topics, on other people and on situations outside the group, while testing the other members and the moderator.

Therefore, the opening question following the introduction to the focus group must be simple, easy to answer, usually descriptive, not too personal, and non-controversial (as indicated in Section 4). The opening question will help to break the ice and get all participants to say something, while also drawing out areas of commonality among the participants (the participants are residents in the same area, for example).

Examples of opening questions

'I would like you to introduce yourselves by telling me your name and where you live.'
'I would like to briefly go around and have each of you say something about how you feel about being here today.'

The moderator will then begin to focus on the topic guide, typically by moving from more general to more specific questions and issues. This 'funnel approach' to interviewing is quite useful in getting the participants themselves to decide what issues are important enough to be raised. The group discussion begins to move on to what Tuckman describes as the *storming stage*. The first general question about the topic is asked, aimed to foster discussion, for example: 'What do you like about your neighbourhood?' 'Are you familiar with equal opportunities guidelines in your workplace?' Participants may still test each other, and will not feel part of the team yet, but they start communicating their views and feelings. At the same time, participants will be concerned with creating an impression of what type of person they are, for instance, intelligent or sceptical. At this stage, there is likely to be competition and conflict (sometimes evident, sometimes not) over claims and opinions, and also over leadership, power and authority.

Competition and conflict affect the interaction, and often some participants will try to dominate the discussion, while others will remain silent. Although competition can have its benefits, you will need to deal with dominant and silent participants as early as possible in the discussion. To do this, you need some controlling techniques, such as those suggested by Krueger for dealing with the problems presented by types such as 'the self-appointed expert', 'the dominant talker', 'the shy participant' and 'the rambler' (1994, p.118). To begin with, you may have to remind the group again that all points of view are important and necessary. You can discourage the self-appointed expert, the dominant participant and the rambler by avoiding eye-contact with them or not acknowledging their contributions, by calling on other participants, and by carefully-worded questions. For example, following a comment, you may say, 'That's very interesting, perhaps we could talk about …' and move on. Alternatively, you can address questions such as the following to the whole group:

Examples of dealing with dominant participants

'Are there any other points of view on this question?'
'Does anyone see it differently?'
'Thank you for that point of view. Does anyone have another?'
'That's helpful. Now let's hear some different thoughts.'

Eye-contact can also be used to encourage shy individuals to express their views. Additional techniques that can help here include head nodding, if it is not excessive and is consciously used, probing and pauses (discussed further below), and using minimal responses, such as 'Yes', 'Right', 'OK', 'Uh-huh'. Be careful, however, to avoid value judgements or expressing preference for certain views. As said earlier, it is better to avoid using responses such as 'Good', 'Correct' or 'Excellent'. These may lead to bias, as people may keep trying to make comments similar to those that received praise by the moderator (Krueger 1994).

Questions such as those in the previous box of examples are designed to get all the participants involved as much as possible and to allow for different viewpoints to be expressed and followed up. As a moderator you will have to work hard to achieve this goal throughout the session, and certainly not only in dealing with dominant, over-talkative or shy participants. Remember that there is often a tendency for people to agree in focus groups, which makes it necessary to encourage alternative and opposing viewpoints: for example, by making a point such as, 'Some people would say ...' Here are some more ways of doing this:

Examples of encouraging different viewpoints

'What do others think about...?'
'Do others agree with...?'
'Do you recognize...?'
'Is this familiar?'
'I see some of you nodding...'
'You don't seem to agree with...'
'Are there any other points of view on this?'
'Does anyone see it differently?'

In addition to questions like these, moderators often use discussion aids to bring out different viewpoints within the group. These are usually projective techniques that encourage participants to make associations between familiar and new stimuli and share their feelings about them (Greenbaum 1998). They include sentence completion tasks, where participants are asked to complete a sentence such as, 'The best thing about this scenario is ...'; word associations; personality associations and situational associations, where photographs of people in certain situations or places may be used to stimulate thinking and elicit a response (for example, in finding out which types of people may choose a product, service or activity); forced relationships, where participants relate images of animals, colours, food and so on to the topic discussed; and asking people to do role-playing, tell a story, visualize a situation or make a drawing that represents an idea or situation.

All these techniques are valuable because they are non-directive, they allow for agreement and disagreement to be expressed in non-threatening and often entertaining ways, and they have the added advantage of involving shy and less articulate individuals. They are also useful for provoking discussion in cases where people may have difficulty bringing up a topic because it is too complex, sensitive or controversial. Finally, presenting people with an ambiguous or incomplete situation (stimulus) allows them to contribute their own interpretation of the situation and their own verbal and non-verbal reactions, while at the same time helping to bypass people's tendency to censor what they say for the sake of social acceptability (Greenbaum 1998).

Let us now continue our discussion of the different stages and dynamics involved in a group discussion, which started with the forming stage. As the group members move more towards problem-solving than competing, the group reaches a *norming stage*. Participants begin to address the issue, acknowledge and value other viewpoints, work together as a team, and solve group issues. As a result of argumentation, counter-argumentation and feedback, participants take on more roles than before, ask questions, and start modifying their own views. The group becomes more cohesive, more effective and more open, with shared leadership and responsibilities (McNamara 1999). To achieve this stage, an atmosphere of openness, support and informality is necessary.

Tuckman also describes an ideal subsequent *performing stage*, when the group works in the most productive and interactive ways to form the debate and redefine the issue. The need for group approval is not strong at this stage, and group loyalty, group identity, trust, flexibility and interdependence will have become more important. As a result, the group develops, personal relations are strengthened and problem solving is achieved.

Your main tasks as the moderator, especially during the key norming and performing stages, will be to keep the discussion flowing and on track, maintain focus and momentum, pay attention to the topic guide and to time, get closure on questions, and keep an equal balance of respondents (for example, by controlling dominant participants). These are different and demanding roles that you are expected to fulfil simultaneously. For example, you should aim to strike a balance between ensuring that all the key topics on the agenda are covered, and allowing adequate time for all participants in the group to respond to each separate question. Also, while it is your responsibility to stop participants from dominating the discussion, breaking the ground rules or having an argument, it will not be beneficial to achieve this by interrupting people – it is better to use some of the techniques mentioned, such as eye-contact, head nodding and minimal responses (see Patton 1990; Krueger 1994). You should also consider using pauses and probes, to which I will now turn.

Pauses and probes can be very useful in soliciting additional information from the group. A short pause after a comment by a participant – often used together with eye-contact from the moderator – can prompt additional comments or an evaluation of a previously expressed position (Krueger 1994). A pause in mid-sentence may be used to add emphasis or to indicate that the speaker has more to say. It may also be used to allow somebody to think more, encourage a new speaker to comment, and offer more opportunity to shy participants to contribute. Probes (introduced at the end of Section 4) are follow-up questions or statements that request additional information. They are useful in getting a participant to reflect and expand on a comment, to clarify vague or complex comments and the links between comments, and to explain, unpack and justify comments. Probes should be simple, clear, focused, and direct (Gillham 2000). The following are common probes used in focus groups:

Examples of probes

'How do you mean this?'
'In what way is this linked to . . .?'/'What is the relationship between . . .?'
'Could you explain further?'
'What makes you say that?'
'How important is that concern?'
'Tell us more about that.'
'Keep talking.'
'Give me a description of what it's like to . . .'
'Would you give me an example of what you mean?'
'Please describe what you mean.'
'What I heard you say was . . .'/'It sounds like you're saying . . .'

> 'I'm wondering how would you deal with a situation in which...?'
> 'What am I missing here?'
> 'Is there anything else?'

Probes can be directed to the whole group as well: for instance, by asking people to contribute their own examples or experiences. 'Does anyone have an example?' and 'Is this anyone else's experience?' are good probes for obtaining further information and for broadening the discussion. Stewart and Shamdasani (1990) recommend against direct probes which ask if anyone agrees or disagrees with the preceding statement. Not only would this be a closed question, but it could also lead to conflict and defensiveness. It is preferable to ask a question such as 'Does anyone see it differently?', or use some of the other ways of opening up the discussion to include multiple viewpoints (mentioned earlier). Finally, another effective way of probing is to reflect on what is being said by repeating or paraphrasing it. This encourages self-reflection and further exploration on the part of the participants, and also lets them know that the moderator is listening (Gillham 2000).

Ten minutes before the end of the session, the moderator should start wrapping up the discussion and alert the group to the amount of time left. Participants gradually stop working on a task and start to disengage from relationships (*adjourning stage*). Ending questions at this stage will close the discussion and allow for reflection by the group members. As described in Section 4, these can be summary or 'all things considered' questions. The summary question is particularly useful, because it gives participants the opportunity to assess the accuracy of the summary of ideas provided by the moderator (Morgan 1993). Once more, when summarizing – at the end, but also every time a major topic has been covered – you should try to use participants' own terms: for example, 'So, people tend to think ...', 'You have mentioned ...', 'You have been talking about ...', 'This goes back to what you were saying ...' The following are common examples of ending questions:

Examples of ending questions

'Of all the ... discussed, which one is most important to you?'
'[...] Is this an adequate summary?'
  And finally:
'Have we missed anything?'
'Would you like to add one last thing?'

The moderator should close the focus group by thanking the participants, providing the gift or cash promised, and assuring them that their comments will be useful and taken seriously. It is important to inform the group of how their comments will be used, and repeat once more what actions you will be taking to ensure anonymity and confidentiality. It is a good idea, and a sign of genuine appreciation of participants' time and effort, to offer to let people have a summary of the results at a later stage, perhaps in the form of a report or an article. This is also an appropriate time to give the group more information and explanation about the purpose of the research, and gauge their reactions. This debriefing exercise is often a stimulus for further discussion that can lead to even further development of existing ideas, and useful new insight (Stewart and Shamdasani 1990).

After the session

Immediately after the session, you should check to see that the tape recorder has worked properly. Together with the assistant moderator or observer, you will need to go through the notes made during the session, making sure that all comments are legible and clear, that diagrams are accurate, and quotes complete. This should take place as soon as possible after the session, ideally on the same or the following day. This also applies to writing down your own observations of the session (Patton 1990), particularly what you felt was striking, surprising, paradoxical, or eloquently put. Immediately after the session, it will be easier to remember such comments and make the links between specific comments and non-verbal behaviour. Finally, it is a good idea to listen through the tapes within days of the session in order to better capture not only what is said on the tape but also the all-important context in which it is said.

The after-session debriefing with the observers is, as discussed, valuable for the analysis of focus group data. You will get immediate reactions following the focus group, helpful insights for analysis, and generally a broader understanding of what happened during the session. You can also benefit from another researcher's perspective, who may have noticed more or different things than you. Observers in my focus groups in the past were able to point to contradictory comments expressed at different stages in the discussion by the same person. For example, one participant was underplaying the moral significance of marriage, while expressing strong moral positions on the topic at other times. The observers were also very insightful about the group dynamics. For example, I was able to confirm, by talking to an observer, that a participant was making attempts to manage the discussion or, in another case, that the men's talk appeared to be less personal, more detached and more general than that of the women (Litosseliti 1999).

It will be equally important, in most projects, to obtain individual participants' views, perceptions and feelings after the focus group. For this purpose, you could administer a questionnaire designed to obtain such personal feedback or, better, conduct brief follow-up interviews with each participant. Follow-up interviews can be conducted in person, depending on location, time and resources. However, I find it as useful to conduct these over the telephone, particularly as the respondents have already invested a lot of time and effort in taking part in a focus group.

Follow-up interviews will give you an opportunity to check factual information that you may have chosen not to obtain during the focus group (for example, participants' age). But most importantly, they are invaluable for getting to participants' own perceptions of the group dynamics as well as views that they may have chosen not to disclose. Some general open-ended questions I have asked in the past were:

Examples of follow-up questions

'How did you think the discussion went?'
'What did you think of the other people in the group?'
'What was it like for you to be in the focus group?'
'Was there anything in the discussion that made you feel uneasy or stopped you from saying something?'
'What did you think about the way the facilitator guided the discussion?'
'What would you change about that focus group?'

Later, these questions tend to become more specific, for example, 'What did you think about the X comment made by Z?' and more directive, for example, 'Did you see any differences in the way men and women talked about marriage?' Sensitive issues and difficulties with communicating in a group situation are likely to be disclosed when you talk to participants one-to-one. I remember two participants once telling me individually that they had been uncomfortable with each other's views during the session, but that they did not want to offend each other by explicitly disagreeing at the time. The follow-up interviews also helped to shed more light on the interaction itself during the sessions, which was a particularly important aspect of my research. For instance, participants identified gender tendencies in interaction – such as men talking more than women, and women talking more openly about personal experience than men – and commented on the levels of agreement and disagreement in the group.

Finally, it is worth asking your participants individually to reflect on the focus group and make suggestions for change or improvement. These will be particularly useful at the beginning of a series of focus groups, as you can then fine tune or revise some of the things you are going to introduce or return to in the next focus group.

Summary

This section described the different stages of a focus group session and provided more specific information and examples on moderating a group. It has suggested that:

- An assistant moderator or observer can be invaluable in focus group research.
- Participants need to be reminded of some ground rules at the beginning of the discussion.
- It is important for the researcher to be aware of the different stages in group discussions (forming, storming, norming, performing, adjourning).
- There are a number of questions, statements, pauses, gestures, projective techniques and probes that can

help the moderator effectively deal with dominant or shy participants, encourage different viewpoints, solicit additional information, and focus or broaden the discussion.

- After a focus group, valuable insight can be gained through debriefing with the observer(s) and through individual follow-up interviews with the participants.

6

Analysing Focus Group Data

In this section, I will look at the most difficult stage of focus group research: analysing the data obtained. The key decisions involved here are about who will do the analysis, the amount of analysis required, and the method of analysis most appropriate for the purposes of the research.

If you are working on a focus group project where you are both the researcher and the moderator, you will most likely also be responsible for analysing the data emerging from the discussions. This gives you the advantage of having more insight and in-context knowledge about the research overall, and so being able to establish a variety of important links between the research questions/aims and the data gathered. While some projects may require a single 'expert' analyst from outside the project, it is advisable that this analyst works closely together with those involved in the planning and running of the groups (researcher, moderator, observers). Similarly, it will be better if the analyst and/or researcher works in collaboration with the transcriber (where a transcriber is hired). Such collaboration will not simply help to identify and clarify gaps in the transcription, but will also lead to a better understanding of the data.

Transcription is one of the issues affected by the amount of analysis required in any focus group project.

You will need to decide whether to transcribe the complete group discussions or whether to use abridged transcripts in analysis. The former can be difficult, slow and time-consuming, but are usually more rigorous and productive than abridged transcripts or a simple debriefing report. As Stewart and Shamdasani (1990) put it: transcripts do not simply provide a record of the discussion, they also allow for a more intimate understanding of the content of the talk, the flow of discussion and the group dynamics, as these emerge linguistically or paralinguistically. My transcripts within the field of linguistics, for example, will always include some description of the important paralinguistic elements of conversation, such as gestures, laughter, sounds of disbelief, gaze and so on. The focus of a lot of linguistic research is on the use of language in context, where how language is used is as important as the words themselves, and therefore for such research more detailed transcription and analysis will be both necessary and fruitful. A summary or report, on the other hand, together with some transcribed examples, may be more appropriate for some projects, depending on the objectives, their complexity, and the questions they aim to address. For example, a report may be adequate when the conclusions of the research are straightforward, when there are time or budget constraints, or when there are very small differences between focus groups. Social science research, however, usually goes beyond a set of decisions or a list of recommendations, to look into reasons, processes, experiences and different kinds of motivations which may require more indepth and more detailed analysis (Stewart and Shamdasani 1990). Also it is important to remember that:

> The data are themselves the result of a unique interaction of moderator and group. Only an understanding of this interaction and the factors

that contribute to it provides a sound basis for the interpretation of focus group data.   (Stewart and Shamdasani 1990, 8)

Another advantage of analysing your own focus groups is that you will be able to think of the analysis of the data as you gather it. Early and continuous analysis of each of a series of focus groups will help you determine the number and focus of subsequent meetings, and will allow you to revise your topic guide or moderating techniques in the light of the information gathered. Allow for a few days between focus groups, in order to be able to carry out some analysis of each discussion before the next. When analysis is understood as continuous – as is the case for most qualitative research – and not something that you do at the end of the collection of information, then several activities can be included in the analytic process. Analysis of the pilot focus group, orientation before the discussion, recorded debriefing with observers after the session and follow-up interviews with participants (see Section 5) are as useful as the more formal analysis of recordings/transcripts and field notes (Dawson, Manderson and Tallo 1993). All these data considered together will aid verification in analysis and help you to avoid the pitfalls of selective perception. Further, comparing your analysis to that carried out by a peer – another researcher who understands the objectives and principles of the study – will also be extremely useful.

Assuming that you will be working with a word-processed transcript, the first step is to read the transcript for general impressions, before gradually looking for specific opinions and topics. You should identify those substantive parts in the transcript that relate to the research questions, as well as any new topics or issues, and classify or code them. This means marking each section of the transcript with code words which describe what participants are talking about, and which are repeated every time an idea or topic reappears. This process can be assisted by using a computer program such as Ethnograph or NUD*IST, which assign designated codes to sections of the text (see an example in Barbour and Kitzinger 1999, Chapter 10). At a later stage in the analysis you may select, review and reframe the coded information in different ways.

The categories to be coded will typically be the result of categories assumed as key by the researchers at the planning of the focus groups, categories which have become evident as key during the discussions, and categories coming up during the actual analysis of the discussions. For example, in their focus groups on heart attack risk factors, Morgan and Spanish (1984) analysed their data on the basis of both what appeared to be key issues during the discussions and what emerged as such during the analysis – a cyclical process. One of the key issues in those interactions turned out to be the asking of questions, and therefore all questions asked among participants were coded, and illustrative quotes were used to show how questions influenced the discussion.

Similarly, in the case of focus groups on the topic of marriage, key categories such as discrimination, cohabitation, change of gender roles, divorce, morality and so on emerged during a back-and-forth or cyclical process of coding and analysis. Let us look at an example of a coded transcript from this research project (Litosseliti 2001):

Transcript extract	Argumentative categories	Gender Assumptions	Linguistic Resources
Steve:/[...] fifty years ago women's expectations were very low or they were very constrained/whereas now they don't see their lives in the same way so. they WON'T put up. and rightly so. they won't put up with a situation where the other partner is constraining them/ that's clearly a key factor in undermining the institution. I mean it MUST be/it's not really people know that divorce is easier or whatever. it's much deeper than that. it's just that people know that they shouldn't put up with it if it isn't working/	Change in gender roles (dominance & tolerance) Change in gender roles as contributing to undermine marriage Divorce	There *has* been a shift in women's expectations It is *women* who have had to 'put up with' unhappy marriages (Power-lessness)	**Time markers**: 'fifty years ago', 'now'. **Contrast**: 'whereas', 'in the same way' **Conviction** about change: present tense verbs (no modals), adverbs ('clearly'), 'it MUST be', **Vagueness**: 'a situation', 'constraining' **Awareness of topic sensitivity; anticipating objection**: 'and rightly so', 'women' – 'people'

Figure 6.1 *Example of a coded transcript with analytical categories*

The example illustrates how analysis is guided by the purpose and objectives of the study. In this case, the objectives were to see how the substantive categories emerging from the data (for example, co-habitation, change of gender roles, divorce, etc.) were used argumentatively, that is, what kind of arguments were being put forward every time these topics were raised. At the same time, the research questions for this study meant that assumptions made by the speakers about gender, and the linguistic resources drawn on in the various arguments, also warranted examination. These simultaneous foci for analysis led to the application of a discourse-analytic framework on the data, examining both the discursive and sociocultural practices of the texts (i.e. the group discussions). As shown in the short example from the transcript above, the text content – the salient themes, arguments and assumptions – is dependant on the text organization – the various linguistic practices and rhetorical strategies – and vice versa. The two are mutually constructed and negotiated (for a more detailed discussion of this relationship, see Litosseliti 2002a; 2002b).

The coding of the data will reflect such analytical decisions. Often, you may begin coding via a content approach, which is then complemented by more qualitative or ethnographic analytical approaches. Content analysis involves identifying the key substantive points in the discussion and categorizing them. The categories need to be exhaustive, in that all substantive statements should fit into a category, and as exclusive as possible, in that statements fit one rather than many categories (Gillham 2000). But, importantly, the analysis of content is an interpretative approach; or rather, your role as a researcher and analyst covers a continuum with the gathering of raw data on one extreme, and the formulating of interpretative comments on the other (Krueger 1994). In interpreting participants' statements, you will also be involved in selecting illustrative examples of data. Again, the selection should reflect the purposes of the study: whether, for example, the aim is to include many diverse comments, to draw attention to usual responses, or to highlight unusual, atypical approaches to a topic. Then, in the writing-up phase, you will use different examples/quotations under different headings, whether these headings correspond to the questions asked during the focus group or to the categories that emerged from the coding of the data. Instead of all quotations, you are likely to use a representative selection of relevant quotations under each heading. This selection may be based on criteria of clarity, intensity or explicitness of quotation, but you should be careful to maintain, as far as possible, a balanced representation, not one that confirms your expectations and ideological presuppositions.

Working with a long transcript – on average of 60 pages – and various pages of field notes is not an easy task. Krueger points out that focus group analysis begins earlier and lasts longer than analysis used in quantitative research. In addition to the volume of data produced, focus group transcripts have multiple meanings and several different interpretations (Holbrook and Jackson 1996). Moreover, researchers have different assumptions and principles of analysis – about systematicity, verification, accessibility and so on. It is therefore important that the analysis is as focused as possible: key or primary questions are of utmost importance for analysis, some questions do not deserve analysis at the same level, while others may be eliminated, as they simply set the background for discussion (Krueger 1994). In addition, be prepared to be flexible about modifying your insights, taking different perspectives and questioning your interpretations during the analysis process. You will need to modify the wording of category headings, shift the content of categories, add new categories and evaluate your interpretations many times during this process. Above all, you will need to be *clear* and *explicit* about these decisions and about the basis for your inferences from the data analysed (Gillham 2000).

More specifically, what should you look for during the analysis process? You will, of course, be examining all participants' comments, looking for the most important themes, issues and ideas. You will be looking for trends and patterns in the content of each discussion, and for similarities and differences across a number of focus groups on the same topic. However, as discussed above, you should not assume that the most important themes and issues are the ones most frequently brought up in the discussion; and similarly, you should be careful not to accept comments at face value. Words and statements can only be considered in context: who articulates them, at what point in the discussion, in response to what comment, in what manner, in association with what kind of non-verbal cues, and within what kind of broader socio-cultural context. This is where full transcripts are particularly helpful for examining the data in depth and detail, and where paying attention to the tapes – including those of the follow-up interviews – and the observer's feedback and field notes can help enhance the analysis. Broadly speaking, the analysis process may involve considering the following:

- Issues, ideas and themes in participants' comments
- Consistencies in behaviour, perceptions, arguments, attitudes
- Inconsistent, contradictory comments and shifts in opinion
- Vague comments versus specific responses
- Context (for example, who makes the comment? Is it based on a prompted example, by the moderator or another participant?)
- Tone (for example, irony) and intensity of comments
- Frequency or extensiveness of an idea (the usefulness or importance of this will depend on the project)
- Balance of positive and negative comments about an issue or idea
- Qualifications and associations made about an issue or idea

- Non-verbal communication (group mood, energy, spontaneity, involvement, body language)

During the complex process of assessing and re-considering these foci, you should, once more, be constantly aware of common analytical mistakes. Bias, previously described as listening for input that confirms the researcher's own beliefs, is a risk also involved in the stage of interpreting the results (Greenbaum 1998). Other common analytical mistakes include generalizing on the basis of participants' individual comments, and quantifying focus group results, when it may be more appropriate to use a small sample for getting to depth, detail and insight. I refer the reader to Section 2, which looks at using focus groups appropriately, and therefore also provides ideas about related analytical assumptions in focus group research. As a reminder, consider the following:

> It is important to keep in mind that the intent of focus groups is not to infer but to understand, not to generalize but to determine the range, not to make statements about the population but to provide insights about how people perceive a situation.
>
> (Krueger 1994, 87)

To return to the analysis, it is not my intention to propose one analytical framework over another, or to go into the complexities of how a specific methodology may treat the foci for analysis listed above. Analytic tools range from simple descriptive analyses to more elaborate techniques (discussed in some of the readings listed at the end of this book; see, in particular, those chapters dealing with analysis in Barbour and Kitzinger 1999). Whatever the methods used, you need to ensure that in-depth analysis of focus group data provides some answers to the following questions:

- Were the objectives achieved?
- What was confirmed and what was challenged by the findings?
- What new ideas emerged?

These questions should be discussed when reporting focus group results in reports and/or academic publications. Focus group reports can be both written and oral. They may consist of a summary of the findings, with recommendations for individuals or organizations, as is often the case with market research. In more academic social science projects, reporting of research outcomes may take the form of an academic article, chapter in a thesis, presentation, report, or a combination of these. Whatever the form and purposes of reporting, the key questions listed above need to be addressed, and the results must be stated clearly, along with their implications – that is, what do the results really mean? At its most basic level, the report should include a summary of the research questions and purpose of the focus groups, the methods used, a profile of the participants, and any other important contextual information, such as the mood in the groups. The main results, ideas, themes and patterns should be presented with appropriate illustrative quotes from the focus groups. This should not simply involve summarizing comments; rather the comments must be linked to hypotheses and patterns, and ultimately to ideas for further research, actions or recommendations. It is also helpful if the person writing the report shares it with the other research team members for review, verification and comment (Krueger 1994).

One other section to include in the report is a comparison between focus groups. As I have mentioned before, the first in a series of focus groups often produces considerable amounts of information, while later groups may not offer much new insight. If this is the case, the

- Were the objectives achieved?
- What was confirmed and what was challenged by the findings?
- What new ideas emerged?

These questions should be discussed when reporting focus group results in reports and/or academic publications. Focus group reports can be both written and oral. They may consist of a summary of the findings, with recommendations for individuals or organizations, as is often the case with market research. In more academic social science projects, reporting of research outcomes may take the form of an academic article, chapter in a thesis, presentation, report, or a combination of these. Whatever the form and purposes of reporting, the key questions listed above need to be addressed, and the results must be stated clearly, along with their implications – that is, what do the results really mean? At its most basic level, the report should include a summary of the research questions and purpose of the focus groups, the methods used, a profile of the participants, and any other important contextual information, such as the mood in the groups. The main results, ideas, themes and patterns should be presented with appropriate illustrative quotes from the focus groups. This should not simply involve summarizing comments; rather the comments must be linked to hypotheses and patterns, and ultimately to ideas for further research, actions or recommendations. It is also helpful if the person writing the report shares it with the other research team members for review, verification and comment (Krueger 1994).

One other section to include in the report is a comparison between focus groups. As I have mentioned before, the first in a series of focus groups often produces considerable amounts of information, while later groups may not offer much new insight. If this is the case, the

asked during the focus group or to the categories that emerged from the coding of the data. Instead of all quotations, you are likely to use a representative selection of relevant quotations under each heading. This selection may be based on criteria of clarity, intensity or explicitness of quotation, but you should be careful to maintain, as far as possible, a balanced representation, not one that confirms your expectations and ideological presuppositions.

Working with a long transcript – on average of 60 pages – and various pages of field notes is not an easy task. Krueger points out that focus group analysis begins earlier and lasts longer than analysis used in quantitative research. In addition to the volume of data produced, focus group transcripts have multiple meanings and several different interpretations (Holbrook and Jackson 1996). Moreover, researchers have different assumptions and principles of analysis – about systematicity, verification, accessibility and so on. It is therefore important that the analysis is as focused as possible: key or primary questions are of utmost importance for analysis, some questions do not deserve analysis at the same level, while others may be eliminated, as they simply set the background for discussion (Krueger 1994). In addition, be prepared to be flexible about modifying your insights, taking different perspectives and questioning your interpretations during the analysis process. You will need to modify the wording of category headings, shift the content of categories, add new categories and evaluate your interpretations many times during this process. Above all, you will need to be *clear* and *explicit* about these decisions and about the basis for your inferences from the data analysed (Gillham 2000).

More specifically, what should you look for during the analysis process? You will, of course, be examining all participants' comments, looking for the most important themes, issues and ideas. You will be looking for trends and patterns in the content of each discussion, and for similarities and differences across a number of focus groups on the same topic. However, as discussed above, you should not assume that the most important themes and issues are the ones most frequently brought up in the discussion; and similarly, you should be careful not to accept comments at face value. Words and statements can only be considered in context: who articulates them, at what point in the discussion, in response to what comment, in what manner, in association with what kind of non-verbal cues, and within what kind of broader socio-cultural context. This is where full transcripts are particularly helpful for examining the data in depth and detail, and where paying attention to the tapes – including those of the follow-up interviews – and the observer's feedback and field notes can help enhance the analysis. Broadly speaking, the analysis process may involve considering the following:

- Issues, ideas and themes in participants' comments
- Consistencies in behaviour, perceptions, arguments, attitudes
- Inconsistent, contradictory comments and shifts in opinion
- Vague comments versus specific responses
- Context (for example, who makes the comment? Is it based on a prompted example, by the moderator or another participant?)
- Tone (for example, irony) and intensity of comments
- Frequency or extensiveness of an idea (the usefulness or importance of this will depend on the project)
- Balance of positive and negative comments about an issue or idea
- Qualifications and associations made about an issue or idea

- Non-verbal communication (group mood, energy, spontaneity, involvement, body language)

During the complex process of assessing and reconsidering these foci, you should, once more, be constantly aware of common analytical mistakes. Bias, previously described as listening for input that confirms the researcher's own beliefs, is a risk also involved in the stage of interpreting the results (Greenbaum 1998). Other common analytical mistakes include generalizing on the basis of participants' individual comments, and quantifying focus group results, when it may be more appropriate to use a small sample for getting to depth, detail and insight. I refer the reader to Section 2, which looks at using focus groups appropriately, and therefore also provides ideas about related analytical assumptions focus group research. As a reminder, consider the following:

It is important to keep in mind that the intent of focus groups is not to infer but to understand, not to generalize but to determine the range, not to make statements about the population but to provide insights about how people perceive a situation.

(Krueger 1994, 87)

To return to the analysis, it is not my intention propose one analytical framework over another, or to into the complexities of how a specific methodology treat the foci for analysis listed above. Analytic tools ra from simple descriptive analyses to more elaborate niques (discussed in some of the readings listed a end of this book; see, in particular, those chapters de with analysis in Barbour and Kitzinger 1999). Wha the methods used, you need to ensure that in-d analysis of focus group data provides some answers following questions:

report should state clearly which results are based on which discussions. In addition, the reporting of results should offer a comparison of all the focus groups, and so include findings that apply to the whole project.

Depending on the project, the research outcomes may be presented to different audiences: the general public, funding bodies, officials, administrators, academics, and so on. A report should be suitable for its target audience, and this will influence its style. For instance, it is better to avoid using jargon with non-researchers. Moreover, you may have to decide whether a narrative or a bullet form of reporting is more appropriate, whether you will use a question/theme and example structure, or a descriptive summary approach to each question followed by interpretation. Generally speaking, there should be a balance between quotations and their summarization and interpretation. A written or oral report must be clear, well-structured and interesting. Using examples and simple tables or diagrams to summarize information for each topic will help achieve this. Most audiences also appreciate identifiable sections for the contents, questions, methods, results, themes, explanations, recommendations and appendices.

Summary

This section discussed key aspects of analysis of focus group data. In particular, it suggested that:

- Analysis must be a collaborative and continuous process among those individuals involved in planning and conducting the focus groups, in cases where the researcher, moderator and analyst are not the same person.

- Different projects will require different levels of transcription and coding and different analytical approaches.
- Analytical categories may emerge from the researcher's early assumptions, during the discussions, and following analysis of the discussions.
- Analysis is always guided by the research question(s) and objectives.
- The various foci for data analysis must be considered in context.
- Any form of reporting of focus group results should address the questions of whether the objectives were achieved, what was confirmed and challenged by the findings, and what new ideas emerged.

Recommended Further Reading

A. General texts on focus group methodology

R. A. Krueger (1994) *Focus Groups: A Practical Guide for Applied Research.*

An excellent accessible book, offering useful examples and guidelines. Krueger takes focus groups outside of marketing research, and puts emphasis on their application to evaluation research.

M. Agar and J. MacDonald (1995) 'Focus Groups and Ethnography', *Human Organization* 54(1).

A study of teenage drug use by two anthropologically-trained ethnographers. Useful for looking at the use of focus groups in conjunction with other ethnographic data, and for finding out about analysis techniques.

T. Greenbaum (1998) *The Handbook for Focus Groups Research.*

A book which looks at focus groups extensively within marketing research. Chapter 6 offers a discussion of using video-conferencing and the Internet for focus groups.

R. Barbour and J. Kitzinger (eds) (1999) *Developing Focus Group Research: Politics, Research and Practice.*

A collection of articles on the theory, practice and politics of focus group research. Particularly useful for its critical thinking around participation and community views, its discussion of often neglected areas (for example, sensitive topics, feminist research), and its useful perspectives on analysis.

M. Bloor *et al.* (2001) *Focus Groups in Social Research.*

An introductory book on the key issues and practical requirements for planning, conducting and analysing focus groups within the social science context. It offers a basic overview of the methodology, and can be used as a supplementary text.

B. Sources on virtual focus groups

There is an abundance of sources on how to conduct online, telephone, video-conferencing and Internet focus groups. In most cases, they are particularly relevant for market researchers.
You can find examples on:

http://www.qualitative-research.net/fqs
http://www.mnav.com/qualitative_research.htm
http://www.groupsplus.com/pags/articles.htm

C. Relevant general texts on research methods

The following texts are selected as valuable guides which take social researchers through the stages of preparing for, carrying out and writing up a research project. They include examples and useful checklists. Texts which may appear out of date (such as Cohen and Manion) are included because they are still both useful and relevant.

L. Cohen and L. Manion (1994) *Research Methods in Education.*

D. Silverman (1993) *Interpreting Qualitative Data: Methods for Analysing Talk, Text, and Interaction.*

D. Rose and O. Sullivan (1996) *Introducing Data Analysis for Social Scientists.*

M. Denscombe (1998) *The Good Research Guide.*

S. Sarantakos (1998) *Social Research.*

J. Bell (1999) *Doing Your Research Project.*

References

Agar, M. and MacDonald, J. (1995) 'Focus groups and ethnography', *Human Organization* 54(1): 78–86.

Barbour, R. and Kitzinger, J. (eds) (1999) *Developing Focus Group Research: Politics, Research and Practice*. London: Sage.

Barker, M. and Brooks, K. (1998) *Knowing Audiences: Judge Dredd, its Friends, Fans and Foes*. Luton: University of Luton Press.

Bell, J. (1999) *Doing your Research Project* (3rd edn). Buckingham: Open University Press.

Bloor, M., Frankland, J., Thomas, M. and Robson, K. (2001) *Focus Groups in Social Research*. London: Sage.

Catterall, M. and Maclaran, P. (1997) 'Focus group data and qualitative analysis programs: Coding the moving picture as well as the snapshots', *Sociological Research Online*, Vol. 2, No. 1. <*http://www.socresonline.org.uk/socresonline/2/1/6.html*>

Cohen, L. and Manion, L. (1994) *Research Methods in Education* (4th edn). London: Routledge.

Dawson, S., Manderson, L. and Tallo, V. (1993) *A Manual for the Use of Focus Groups*. INFDC: Boston, MA.

Denscombe, M. (1998) *The Good Research Guide for Small-scale Social Research Projects*. Buckingham: Open University Press.

Gibbs, A. (1997) 'Focus groups', *Social Research Update*, Issue Nineteen. Department of Sociology, University of Surrey. *<http://www.soc.surrey.ac.uk/sru/SRU19.html>*

Gillham, B. (2000) *The Research Interview*. London: Continuum.

Goss, J. D. and Leinbach, T. R. (1996) 'Focus groups as alternative research practice', *Area* 28(2): 115–23.

Greenbaum, T. (1998) *The Handbook for Focus Group Research*. London: Sage.

Holbrook, B. and Jackson, P. (1996) 'Shopping around: focus group research in North London', *Area* 28(2): 136–42.

Kitzinger, J. (1994) 'The methodology of focus groups: the importance of interaction between research participants', *Sociology of Health* 16(1): 103–21.

Kitzinger, J. (1995) 'Introducing focus groups', *British Medical Journal* 311: 299–302.

Krueger, R. A. (1994) *Focus Groups: a Practical Guide for Applied Research*. London: Sage.

Lamnek, S. (1995) *Qualitative Sozialforschung*. Weinheim: Psychologie-Verlags-Union, Band 2, 3. Aufl.

Lankshear, A. J. (1993) 'The use of focus groups in a study of attitudes to student nurse assessment', *Journal of Advanced Nursing* 18: 1986–89.

Lederman, L. C. (1990) 'Assessing educational effectiveness: The focus group interview as a technique for data collection', *Communication Education*, 39(2): 117–27.

Litosseliti, L. (1999) 'Moral Repertoires and Gender Voices in Argumentation'. PhD thesis, Department of Linguistics and MEL, Lancaster University, UK.

Litosseliti, L. (2001) 'Language, culture and gender identities: Examining arguments about marriage'. In Stroinska, M. (ed.) *Relative Points of View: Linguistic Representations of Culture*, 119–40. London/New York: Berghahn.

Litosseliti, L. (2002a) 'The discursive construction of morality and gender: Investigating public and private arguments'. In Benor, S., Rose, M., Sharma, D., Sweetland, J. and Zhang, Q. (eds) *Gendered Practices in Language*, 45–63. Stanford: Center for the Study of Language and Information, Stanford University.

Litosseliti, L. (2002b) 'Head to head: The construction of morality and gender identity in newspaper arguments'. In Litosseliti, L. and Sunderland, J. (eds) *Discourse Analysis and Gender Identity*, Vol. 2, 129–48. Amsterdam: Benjamins.

Litosseliti, L. and Sunderland, J. (eds.) (2002) *Discourse Analysis and Gender Identity*, Vol. 2. Amsterdam: Benjamins.

Mayring, P. (1993) *Qualitative Inhaltsanalyse*. Aufl., Neuausg. Weinheim: Deutscher Studien-Verlag.

McNamara, C. (1999) 'Group dynamics: Basic nature of groups and how they develop', Center for Service and Leadership, Fairfax, Virginia. *<http://www.mapnp.org/library/grp_skll/theory/theory.htm>*

Merton, R. K. (1987) 'The focussed interview and focus groups: Continuities and discontinuities', *Public Opinion Quarterly* 51(4): 550–66.

Morgan, D. L. (1988) *Focus Groups as Qualitative Research*. London: Sage.

Morgan, D. L. (ed.) (1993) *Successful Focus Groups: Advancing the State of the Art*. Newbury Park, CA: Sage.

Morgan, D. L. (1997) *Focus Groups as Qualitative Research* (2nd edn). London: Sage.

Morgan, D. L. and Krueger, R. A. (1993) 'When to use focus groups and why'. In Morgan, D. L. (ed.) *Successful Focus Groups*. London: Sage.

Morgan, D. L. and Krueger, R. A. (1997) *The Focus Group Kit*. London: Sage.

Morgan, D. L. and Spanish, M. T. (1984) 'Focus groups: A new tool for qualitative research', *Qualitative Sociology* 7: 253–70.

Munodawafa, D., Gwede, C., and Mubayira, C. (1995) 'Using focus groups to develop HIV education among adolescent females in Zimbabwe', *Health Promotion* 10(2): 85–92.

Myers, G. (1998) 'Displaying opinions: Topics and disagreement in focus groups', *Language in Society* 27(1): 85–111.

Myers, G. and Macnaghten, P. (1998) 'Rhetorics of environmental sustainability: Commonplaces and places', *Environment and Planning* A 30(2): 333–53.

Myers, G., Szerszynski, B. and Urry, J. (1996–99) 'Global Citizenship and the Environment'. ESRC research project, Lancaster University, UK.

O'Brien, K. (1993) 'Improving survey questionnaires through focus groups'. In Morgan D. (ed.) *Successful Focus Groups: Advancing the State of the Art.* 105–18. London: Sage.

Patton, M. (1990) *Qualitative Evaluation and Research Methods* (2nd edn). Newbury Park, CA: Sage.

Powell, R. A. and Single, H. M. (1996) 'Focus groups', *International Journal of Quality in Health Care* 8(5): 499–504.

Race, K. E., Hotch, D. F. and Parker, T. (1994) 'Rehabilitation program evaluation: use of focus groups to empower clients', *Evaluation Review* 18(6): 730–40.

Rezabek, R. (2000) 'Online focus groups: Electronic discussions for research', *Forum Qualitative Sozialforschung / Forum: Qualitative Social Research* [On-line Journal], 1(1). *<http://qualitative-research.net/fqs>*

Rose, D. and Sullivan, O. (1996) *Introducing Data Analysis for Social Scientists* (2nd edn). Buckingham: Open University Press.

Sarantakos, S. (1998) *Social Research* (2nd edn). South Melbourne: Macmillan

Silverman, D. (1993) *Interpreting Qualitative Data: Methods for Analysing Talk, Text, and Interaction.* London: Sage.

Silverman, G. (2000) 'Everything in moderation', *The Market Navigator Newsletter,* Vol. 1, No. 5. *<http://www.mnav.com/evmod.htm>*

Skeggs, B., Moran, L. and Truman, C. (1998–2000) *Violence, Security, Space: A Study of the Practical and Policy Context of Substantive Safe Public Spaces.* ESRC research project. Lancaster University, UK.

Stewart, D. W. and Shamdasani, P. N. (1990) *Focus Groups: Theory and Practice.* London: Sage.

Templeton, J. (1987) *Focus Groups: A Guide for Marketing and Advertising Professionals.* Chicago: Probus.

Tuckman, B. (1965) 'Developmental sequence in small groups', *Psychological Bulletin* 63: 384–99.

Tuckman, B. and Jensen, M. (1977) 'Stages of small group development', *Group and Organizational Studies* 2: 419–27.

Wells, W. D. (1974) 'Group interviewing'. In Ferber, R. (ed.), *Handbook of Marketing Research.* New York: McGraw-Hill.

Wilkinson, S. (1998) 'Focus groups – A feminist method', *Psychology of Women Quarterly* 23(2): 221–44.

Wilkinson, S. (1999) 'How useful are focus groups in feminist research?' In Barbour, R. and Kitzinger, J. (eds) *Developing Focus Group Research: Politics, Research and Practice,* 64–78. London: Sage.

Wodak, R., de Cillia, M. and Liebhart, K. (1999) *The Discursive Construction of National Identity.* Edinburgh: Edinburgh University Press.